Your Horoscope 2021

Capricorn

22 December – 20 January

igloobooks

Published in 2020
by Igloo Books Ltd
Cottage Farm
Sywell
NN6 0BJ
www.igloobooks.com

0820 001
2 4 6 8 10 9 7 5 3 1
ISBN 978-1-83852-316-9

Written by Belinda Campbell and Denise Evans

Cover design by Simon Parker
Edited by Bobby Newlyn-Jones

Printed and manufactured in China

CONTENTS
. . . .

INTRODUCTION

. . . .

This 15-month guide has been designed and written to give a concise and accessible insight into both the nature of your star sign and the year ahead. Divided into two main sections, the first section of this guide will give you an overview of your character in order to help you understand how you think, perceive the world and interact with others and – perhaps just as importantly – why. You'll soon see that your zodiac sign is not just affected by a few stars in the sky, but by planets, elements, and a whole host of other factors, too.

The second section of this guide is made up of daily forecasts. Use these to increase your awareness of what might appear on your horizon so that you're better equipped to deal with the days ahead. While this should never be used to dictate your life, it can be useful to see how your energies might be affected or influenced, which in turn can help you prepare for what life might throw your way.

By the end of these 15 months, these two sections should have given you a deeper understanding and awareness of yourself and, in turn, the world around you. There are never any definite certainties, but with an open mind you will find guidance for what might be, and learn to take more control of your own destiny.

THE CHARACTER OF
THE SEA GOAT
. . . .

One small step for Capricorn can certainly be one giant leap
for mankind when this determined sign gets its teeth into
something. Whether it's dreaming of the stars like Capricorns
Buzz Aldrin and Stephen Hawking or striving for first place
like Tiger Woods, Capricorns are the earth signs of the
calendar that can make their dreams a reality. Belonging to the
tenth house of the zodiac calendar where careers and vocations
are key, the role that a disciplined Capricorn takes on, be it in
business, science, or on the stage, can take them to dizzying
heights of success. As an earth sign, tangible rewards can be
essential to Capricorns — just look at their designer clothes,
nice cars and beautiful houses — and if a Capricorn hasn't
quite reached their goals yet, their dreams of grandeur will
likely inspire them to only work harder.

Born with buckets of ambition, the Goat-symbolised Capricorn
will not be satisfied with climbing mere ladders and will likely
set themselves mountains to ascend. If the path they have
taken is proving to be too rocky, rejection and failure can hit
this prideful sign hard and any pain might be internalised due
to their negative nature. Capricorns are pioneering cardinal
characters, and the world can be more than happy to dance
to their Pied Piper tune. Just look at Calvin Harris, a Forbes-
listed Capricorn recorded for being the highest paid DJ in the
world for six consecutive years, showing how hardworking
Capricorns can not only reach but stay at the top of their
profession. Status is of all importance to Capricorns so being
top dog, or Sea Goat rather, could be what helps drive this sign
to the highest peaks of their success. Their top-of-the-podium
seeking attitude is perhaps why the number one and number

two spots for the record amount of Formula 1 wins are both held by Capricorns: Michael Schumacher and Lewis Hamilton. Whatever their goals are, with authoritative Saturn ruling over Capricorn, this disciplined sign is sure to get results.

THE SEA GOAT

Often depicted as a mountain Goat with the tail of a fish, Capricorns are the practical and creative doers of the zodiac calendar. With the sure-footed hooves of the Goat, Capricorns can approach their goals with perseverance and authority whilst their fishy tail suggests that they may also have a creative and sensitive side hiding beneath their stoic features. Earth sign Capricorns will usually find comfort in solid things and enjoy following a clear path that has tangible rewards at the end of it. This Goat isn't about taking the easy route though, Capricorns can be found confidently scaling the trickiest and longest paths with their stubbornly hard-working attitude. Born at the start of winter, the Goat is happy to take the path less trodden and seek out their own way in life, which can give them a reputation being a loner to some extent. The Goat can be a serious soul thanks to their authoritative planet of Saturn so would do well to try and lighten up from time to time and remember what it was like to be a kid again.

SATURN

The second largest planet in the Solar System, Saturn rules over the eye-catching Capricorn. Dead set on achieving their goals, this ground-breaking earth sign is likely to be well known in whatever they choose to do in their lives. Named after the Roman god of agriculture, Saturn-led Capricorns can be wonderful at sowing a seed, working the earth and watching the abundant fruits of their labour grow to fruition. Despite Saturday being the namesake of Capricorn's ruling planet, this Saturn sign can struggle to say goodbye to their work and hello to the weekend. The planet of authority and discipline might not make Saturn an obvious choice for kicking off a fun-filled weekend, however, it is a forced reminder that breaks must be taken and marks a tradition that even this sign can't ignore. For Capricorns, taking time away from their work can be tough so their ruling planet, Saturn, can act as an important reminder that all work and no play makes Capricorn as useful as a dull blade.

ELEMENTS, MODES AND POLARITIES

Each sign is made up of a unique combination of three defining groups: elements, modes and polarities. Each of these defining parts can manifest in good and bad ways, and none should be seen to be a positive or a negative — including the polarities! Just like a jigsaw puzzle, piecing these groups together can help illuminate why each sign has certain characteristics and help us find a balance.

ELEMENTS

Fire: Dynamic and adventurous, signs with fire in them can be extroverted. Others are naturally drawn to them because of the positive light they give off, as well as their high levels of energy and confidence.

Earth: Signs with the earth element are steady and driven with their ambitions. They make for a solid friend, parent or partner due to their grounded influence and nurturing nature.

Air: The invisible element that influences each of the other elements significantly, air signs will provide much-needed perspective to others with their fair thinking, verbal skills and key ideas.

Water: Warm in the shallows and freezing as ice. This mysterious element is essential to the growth of everything around it, through its emotional depth and empathy.

MODES

Cardinal: Pioneers of the calendar, cardinal signs jump-start each season and are the energetic go-getters.

Fixed: Marking the middle of the calendar, fixed signs firmly denote and value steadiness and reliability.

Mutable: As the seasons end, the mutable signs adapt and give themselves over gladly to the promise of change.

POLARITIES

Positive: Typically extroverted, positive signs take physical action and embrace outside stimulus in their life.

Negative: Usually introverted, negative signs value emotional development and experiencing life from the inside out.

CAPRICORN IN BRIEF

The table below shows the key attributes of Capricorn.
Use it for quick reference and to understand more about this fascinating sign.

SYMBOL	RULING PLANET	MODE	ELEMENT	HOUSE
The Sea Goat	Saturn	Cardinal	Earth	Tenth

COLOUR	BODY PART	POLARITY	GENDER	POLAR SIGN
Brown	Joints, Bones and Teeth	Negative	Feminine	Cancer

ROMANTIC RELATIONSHIPS

. . . .

Despite Capricorn's fishy tail suggesting a sensitive side seen in water signs, it's unlikely that this earth sign will feel all that comfortable with emotional displays of affection. When a Capricorn wants to express to their other half just how much they mean to them, it may be by way of physical gifts, like a box of expensive chocolates or even a new car. The greatest romantic gift for a Capricorn will usually be an engagement ring, as marriage will be essential to many of this sign, partly due to their desire for security and their value of upholding tradition. Giving a partner emotional support and stability can be essential in any relationship, however, for the pragmatic Capricorn who can be too focused on providing financial security for their loved ones, this can at times be forgotten. If a Capricorn is in the habit of showing their love by ways of expensive present giving, they should remember that gifts of the greatest value do not always have the highest price tags.

Born in the tenth house in the zodiac calendar that focuses on careers and vocation, a Capricorn can be guilty of prioritising their work above their relationship. For a Capricorn, they may view the long hours that they are spending at the office as a sacrifice that they are happy to make for their partner in order to provide them with a beautiful home, money for holidays, or expensive cars. Whilst a Capricorn is unlikely to be deliberately neglecting their partner, usually being highly devoted in their relationships, establishing a balance between home life and work life can be essential to Capricorns finding long-term happiness in love. Finding a playful partner that can coax this Goat sign out from their desk of solitude and persuade them to relax and enjoy life is key for Capricorns in love.

ARIES: COMPATIBILITY 1/5

The cynical Capricorn is not an obvious lover for ambitious Aries but shouldn't necessarily be ruled out entirely as a potential partner. Capricorns usually take longer to make up their mind about a partner than the quick-working Aries, so Aries will need to exert some patience and work at Capricorn's slower pace if they want this challenging relationship to work. Like with any relationships, their differences can be their strengths. Be mindful of not wanting to change each other and learn how each can make the other a better, more well-rounded, person.

TAURUS: COMPATIBILITY 3/5

Capricorn and Taurus in love are loyal and true to each other. These two earth signs value hard work and are driven by their need to enjoy the fruits of their labours. The home that these two could build together will likely be full of beautiful and expensive objects, with a couple of prized cars jewelling their garage. Whilst both will have dreams of marriage, Capricorn is the more traditional one and will probably approach the subject first. Taurus should try to inject joy and fun into the relationship to teach Capricorn to enjoy the lighter side of life.

GEMINI: COMPATIBILITY 1/5

This earth and air coupling between Capricorn and Gemini may be an unlikely match but awareness of their differences could help create a stronger bond. Capricorns appreciate the tangible: a good career and beautiful home, whilst Geminis love exciting ideas and the invisible workings of the mind. Whilst a Gemini's mutable element fits well with the cardinal aspect of Capricorn, what drives Capricorn may be at odds with the interests of Gemini. This polar opposite couple, Capricorn negative and Gemini positive, may struggle to find common ground but could stand to learn the most from one another.

CANCER: COMPATIBILITY 5/5

Opposites on the zodiac calendar, Capricorn and Cancer can experience a tenacious love. When water sign Cancer rains down on earth sign Capricorn they can create a beautiful life together. Symbolised often with a fish's tail, the Sea Goat that represents Capricorn can swim happily in a Cancerian's warm waters. A Cancerian can indeed help coax a playfulness in Capricorn that others don't always see. Capricorns are ruled by the authoritative planet of Saturn so could be a strong parenting partner for the family orientated Cancerian. If these two hard-working signs fall in love with each other, the dedication that they share could be staggering.

LEO: COMPATIBILITY 4/5

Leo and Capricorn are the success story of when opposites can attract in love. Both these signs tend to have a clear sense of purpose, for Leo it is in their personal life goals and for Capricorn a clear career path is their focus. Leo Barack Obama and Capricorn Michelle Obama are an ideal example of how well these two can work towards achieving their dreams together. Capricorn can show Leo what hard work can accomplish, and Leo can bring the fun that sometimes the cool and dignified Capricorn can be lacking. Leo and Capricorn are two strong characters that can be even stronger together.

VIRGO: COMPATIBILITY 4/5

When the hard-working Capricorn and meticulous Virgo fall in love, there won't be many cracks in their relationship. With a Virgo's toolkit of organisation and practical skills and a Capricorn's portfolio of material achievements, this hard-working couple may be great at taking on exciting and grand projects together. Perhaps building their own home somewhere in the countryside would suit this couple, where their shared earth element can be appreciated at its best, and their quieter negative energies embraced. This firm relationship may lack some spontaneity, so thoughtful surprises now and again could help keep their home fires burning.

LIBRA: COMPATIBILITY 1/5

The firm footed Goat of Capricorn and high-spirited air sign of Libra could have little shared ground and struggle to strike a balance in love, but a relationship should not be ruled out. Born in the seventh house of relationships, Libras may struggle if Capricorns, born in the tenth house of careers, put their job before their partnership, so finding a middle ground between work and personal life will be essential for a happy union. It could be hard to find equality for this earth and air match when their differences are so vast, however, their commitment could well outweigh any differences.

SCORPIO: COMPATIBILITY 5/5

When Capricorn and Scorpio set their sights on each other, these highly dedicated signs could be in it for the long run. Placed two apart on the zodiac calendar, theirs is a devout bond that is likely to be highly compatible with matching negative energies, complementary elements, and strong cardinal and fixed modes. A Capricorn can offer the security that Scorpio desires and Scorpio can be the powerful influence that feeds Capricorn's ambition. Scorpio will bring the fun and Capricorn will bring the itinerary to go with it. If they can take it in turns to rule the roost, their love could go the distance.

SAGITTARIUS: COMPATIBILITY 2/5

A materialist Capricorn and dazzling Sagittarius can both be guilty of feeling a little superior, which won't do in a partnership, especially when these two can have such different approaches to life. The rational Capricorn may be fearful of going to daring heights with their lively Sagittarius partner but if they are open to Sagittarian's optimism, they could learn to love more bravely. A Sagittarius may feel constrained by Capricorn's constant reminder that actions have consequences but looking before they leap could be a vital lesson that a Capricorn teaches their Sagittarian partner. The key to their happiness may be embracing each other's opposites.

CAPRICORN: COMPATIBILITY 3/5

Through better and through worse, there's probably no peak that these two Goats could not reach together. When a cardinal couple like two Capricorns fall in love, their accomplishments can be great, however, arguments over who is the driver in this partnership can cause rifts. Like any long journey or long-term relationship, it's all about taking turns behind the wheel; someone should remember to bring the car games as fun may be forgotten by this serious pair. Both earth signs, these two may be focused on material things but they are also devoted and grounded partners to one another.

AQUARIUS: COMPATIBILITY 1/5

Both ruled by Saturn, Capricorns and Aquarians will usually have a good understanding of the rules of love, however, Aquarians are co-ruled by Uranus so may rebel against the traditions that most Capricorns value. A Capricorn and an Aquarius can both be extremely independent people which may be what attracts them to one another, and as a creative couple they can really bring out the best in each other. This is a union of strong personalities and beliefs that may struggle to find common ground due to their opposite negative and positive energies, although their differences and determination could be their success.

PISCES: COMPATIBILITY 3/5

An earth and water love is bound to be a complementary match, and the relationship with a Capricorn and Piscean may be about helping each other grow as individuals and flourish as a couple. Capricorn will bring a practical mind and an active spirit with their cardinal nature whilst the mutable Piscean will provide compassion and teach their Goat to be flexible. Both sides can retreat into themselves in times of great focus or reflection, particularly Pisceans if their Goat partner is being overbearing. However, their matching negative energies could form a deep emotional connection with each other and demonstrate true patience and dedication.

FAMILY AND FRIENDS

Capricorns are the hard workers of the zodiac calendar, and a big driving force as to why they work so hard can be their family. A Capricorn may have ambitions of being the provider to their loved ones, providing food on the table, money for school trips, and a nice roof over their heads. Capricorns are usually house-proud individuals and for good reason, with their traditional taste and appreciation of materials, their house may have original beam features or luxurious sofas that show off their love for sturdy and tangible objects. Building a solid and secure home life for their family may be a Capricorn's dream and their self-sufficiency and drive can make them determined not to rely on others. Capricorns should be careful of becoming too focused on their work life and neglecting their home life as they might find that they start to alienate themselves from their loved ones if they do so. Sharing responsibilities will free them up to enjoy the fruits of their labours and the real treasures in their life, which for homebody Capricorn is truly their family.

Like everything else in a Capricorn's life, friendships too may be measured by their value. For some cool kids, this cardinal Goat sign may seek out friendships that they believe will advance their social status further, as is their talent for sniffing out a solid investment. Whilst Capricorns love having control over their destiny, this sign would do well to leave the strategising in their financial lives, and out of their friendships if they don't want to get a reputation of using people for their own personal gain. When Capricorns take a day off from planning their empires, they may find that the unexpected or oldest friendships this sign has are the most rewarding and worth investing more time in. Capricorns are a steady force of friendship, ready to support their loved ones through good times and bad. But they may not always be as receptive to help from their friends. Positive and high energy signs like Leo and Sagittarius can help Capricorns loosen up and learn to not just live life to its maximum but to have fun whilst doing so too.

As a child, parents can be the first and key figure of authority in most people's lives, however, for Saturn ruled Capricorn, their first experience of discipline and establishing boundaries can be even more relevant. Should a Capricorn have their own children, or look after other people's children, their Saturn influence will mean that their deep-set feelings of responsibility may make them a strict parent or guardian as they will not take these duties lightly. Setting curfews, dishing out chores, and checking homework could be jobs that the Capricorn parent takes in their stride. Capricorns may also want to teach their child practical skills like learning to drive or riding a bike and will no doubt take huge pride in witnessing and being part of their children's achievements.

MONEY AND CAREERS

. . . .

Being a certain star sign will not dictate the type of career that you have, although the characteristics that fall under each sign could help you identify the areas in which you could potentially thrive. Conversely, to succeed in the workplace, it is just as important to understand what you are good at as it is to know what you are less brilliant at so that you can see the areas in which you will need to perhaps work harder in to achieve your career and financial goals.

Belonging to the tenth house where occupation and vocation are everything, it is no wonder that this sign has a great chance of rising up the ranks in their chosen profession. As a cardinal sign ruled by the authoritative planet of Saturn, Capricorns can suit high-powered and high-earning jobs as a director or CEO of a company. Ambition is Capricorn's middle name and thanks to their cardinal nature, their drive for success can see them become trailblazers in their professional field. Trendsetting designer Diane von Fürstenberg, activist leader Martin Luther King Jr., and pioneer of glam rock David Bowie are all Capricorns that have lit the way for others to follow by climbing their personal ladders to success. Whatever this Sea Goat sets their mind to, Capricorn's tenacity teamed with their strong will means that whilst they may take a while getting wherever they are going, their destination will be worth it. They will not be afraid of being different, nor will they apologise for forging new paths - Capricorns know who they are and where they want to be, so work hard to achieve their goals.

MONEY AND CAREERS

Capricorns are one of the earth signs of the zodiac, so tangible objects can bring this sign great satisfaction. Certificates, trophies and medals will usually adorn Capricorns' walls, shelves and neck, as a visual reminder of the greatness that they can achieve. Careers where a Capricorn can use their practical skills, perhaps as a property developer or learning a specific trade may suit this sign as it could satisfy their need for material things and provide them with a solid outcome and income from their hard work. Capricorns are usually careful with money, apart from when they are trying to impress someone, in which cases they may be caught spending beyond their means in order to try and make a good impression. Whilst Capricorns may be seen to splurge, any expenses that this sign makes will be judged on what they will receive in return, so a Capricorn will probably view their spending more as investing. The returns may not always be monetary, but Capricorns will value appreciation of their gifts.

Whilst you can't always choose who you work with, it can be advantageous to learn about colleagues' key characteristics through their star signs to try and work out the best ways of working with them. Like Capricorns, Virgos can be wonderful planners, so these to-do list lovers could very well be responsible for overseeing the Christmas work do or co-presenting at important meetings together, managing projects with precision and panache. Taureans can work doggedly with hard-working Capricorns through the most difficult of tasks, and will bond over their shared grit and determination to see tasks through to the end even if the odds seem to be against them. Capricorn's cardinal nature can mean that they are happy to work on their own and may clash with other cardinal signs in a contest for power, however, inspiring Aries and passionate Cancerians can make for stimulating cardinal colleagues.

HEALTH AND WELLBEING

. . . .

When you are as adept at climbing so many ladders in life, overcoming obstacles and conquering mountains like the Goat in Capricorn is, you may also find that you have the legs for great physical challenges. Running marathons, cycling on rocky terrains, or mountaineering could all be challenges the sporty Capricorn enjoys, and if there is a shiny medal or trophy to be won at the end of it, then all the better for this magpie sign. Associated with joints and bones, Capricorns may like to pay extra attention to looking after these areas of the body. So once this mountain Goat has picked up their medals for their sporting achievements, taking the time to unwind with some yoga stretches will no doubt help keep their tired joints from seizing up on them. Eating a balanced diet rich in omega-3 from plenty of fish and nuts could help keep joints loose and well-oiled whilst taking relevant supplements could also put the pep back into a Capricorn's step.

Capricorns can be oh-so serious, worrying about this or that and planning everything within an inch of its life so that they achieve the staggering excellence that they are after. But striving for success, whilst being a motivational force, can at times be a tough burden to bear, particularly if a Capricorn's dreams aren't going to plan. This sign can have a reputation for being pessimistic in their pragmatic approach to life, and their grumbling can lead to moaning which can leave them with a cold and hard view of the world. Indeed, when life gives Capricorn lemons, the severe disappointment that they are left with can make it hard to see how exactly they can make lemonade. For a sign that likes to feel sure-footed, not knowing where they stand can rattle this sign and leave them feeling unsteady and uneasy. Control might not be an easy thing for Capricorns to let go of, but the sooner this sign accepts that certain things cannot be predicted, the sooner they can relax and enjoy the unknown.

Keeping Capricorn's health and wellbeing in check may be linked to keeping their work and personal life balanced. Too often, a Capricorn can put their work duties ahead of their health and happiness by working themselves to the bone on a regular basis. A Capricorn may feel better initially by staying late in the office or answering work emails at the weekend as a way of staying on top of their heavy workloads, however, working endlessly is not sustainable for any sign and a burnout could be just around the corner if this sign is not careful. Capricorns' work ethics can be admirable, but they can be so fixed on their end goal that they may not see that the journey is damaging their health and wellbeing. The key for Capricorns may be to rest just as hard as they work, as all work and no downtime is never good for any sign.

Capricorn

....

DAILY FORECASTS
for 2020

OCTOBER

. . . .

Thursday 1st

October kicks off with the Full Moon in Aries. This places
everything relating to home and family in the spotlight. It's an
area that's been highlighted for some time since Mars entered
and it will continue to be an area of focus for the remainder of
2020. What is your inner child wanting you to see?

Friday 2nd

Venus comes into Virgo. She doesn't really like to be here, as
everything has to be too perfect and too real but, as the ruler
of Taurus, she is familiar with the earth element and can
support your energy a lot. If you want to add a sense of value
and beauty to your visions, this is a great time to do it.

Saturday 3rd

You should be feeling the arrival and benefit of happy planetary
energy – Moon in Taurus connects to Venus, and they are
sending good vibes to you. You should feel a wonderful sense
of stability and may have a lot of fun in letting your creativity
play. The energy is also breathing life into your travel plans.

Sunday 4th

There should still be a flowing feeling but a sudden question
can arise regarding what is yours and what belongs to others.
While engaging in a group setting, are you still following your
own ideas or are you falling into a herd mentality? Make sure
you access all of your inner resources; you have plenty.

Monday 5th

While you tap into your creative potential, Pluto the great transformer and destroyer has done enough deconditioning for now and moves direct again. This marks the beginning of a powerful time in which you select what bits and pieces can be reintegrated and which ones are gone for good. You should find greater clarity in terms of which projects to focus you energies on right now.

Tuesday 6th

The Moon in Gemini flows with the Sun in Libra. You are in a busy frame of mind, which is fantastic for getting things done. If you choose challenging tasks, you will have time and energy to get them completed. You should have faith that you already have all the resources you require at this time.

Wednesday 7th

Keep your ears fully open today. There is a piece of information coming in that can totally alter your perspective, and this may come from somewhere unexpected. This could come from an everyday situation, such as hearing a piece of conversation or something catching your eye. Pay particular attention to what friends have to say.

Thursday 8th

It's likely to be another productive day where you check off your to-do list like a pro. By the end of the day, you may feel your mood shift and feel happy to sink into the nurturing arms of your partner. The to-do list can be forgotten, and you should enjoy revelling in togetherness.

Friday 9th

There's still lots of love in the air and no matter how long you have been with your partner or whether or not you are married, you might want to plan a honeymoon of a sort. Maybe it's the desire to just get away for a while, at least for a moment?

Saturday 10th

A spontaneous trip or event might take place. You might wake up to packed bags or find yourself at the airport taking a last-minute flight. Alternatively, you might find yourself taking a small break from the everyday. Whatever the case, this hiatus is probably related to wellness or exploring or both. If a heart is happy, so is the soul.

Sunday 11th

It's a day to enjoy but also to be careful not to overindulge or dramatise, or to connect to too many people. Every time you turn around there could be another trap. Jupiter's downside of overstepping boundaries, or overdoing things, can show up. Too much of a good thing can have negative consequences, so try to exercise moderation.

Monday 12th

It's hard to believe, but you might not want to go to work today. If you're lucky then you may already be on a break, but you may also find something that's not the way you like it and throw a temper tantrum or two. Don't take yourself so seriously.

Tuesday 13th

The Sun and Mars are facing each other and the theme of the Full Moon is echoed. Once again, you need to find balance, as no side has all the advantages. You are able to take a thorough look at all the details but will probably have to wait to act upon them.

Wednesday 14th

Mercury retrograde is back. There's a deep need to reflect on all the information received recently, and you turn into an investigative detective to find what has been hidden. Use the next few weeks for deep conversations with your friends, and they will assist you in getting to the bottom of the situation.

Thursday 15th

The Sun has another discussion with Pluto and you might find yourself in a power struggle. You could be faced with an authority figure, or you could be the authority figure in charge. In both cases, it's about the fair use of the power that is being wielded. Holding power asks for responsibility and integrity.

Friday 16th

Happy New Moon in Libra. Now would be a great time to set new goals for your career and vocation. The central need is to retain or establish integrity. How do you want to appear in the world, and how do you want to be perceived? How much power do you desire? A good look inward may help you navigate the outward world.

. . . .

Saturday 17th

Your emotions and thoughts align today in the depth of the realm of Scorpio. Nothing superficial can touch you, and every answer you find will lead to another question. At least one of your findings will trigger an unexpected emotional response, either from you or another person. Take that into account.

Sunday 18th

A sense of responsibility, trustworthiness and integrity are some of the values connected to Capricorn. Are you also just, merciful and non-judgemental? Today, you might want to ponder how many of these traits you have embodied so far. It is helpful to ask how others perceive you. Your friends can help you reflect on that.

Monday 19th

With a great sense of reality you can estimate how far you can stretch the boundaries, but what happens if you cross them? It can lead to a conflict within your home or an inner conflict regarding your beliefs. If you don't want to talk it through with anyone, then draw back and seek a connection with nature.

Tuesday 20th

From the depths of your subconscious, an old belief might rise to the surface. You might wonder about it or you might be cynical. Remember, whenever you become conscious of something, it is an invitation to integrate it as part of your identity. If the belief you have remembered doesn't serve you, release it.

Wednesday 21st

The right things are starting to happen at the right times. Or at least some of the time, anyway. Venus, in a flowing connection to Pluto, is showing the transformation inside you. You are also integrating the new things that you have learned. It is another stepping stone to the future.

Thursday 22nd

The depth of Scorpio season is knocking on your door as the Sun is entering your area of friends, communities, hopes and wishes. It's about your deepest desires and with whom you share them. It's about engaging in a trustworthy tribe. Are you willing to stop climbing higher for a little while, to dive a little deeper?

Friday 23rd

For you to trust somebody, it's essential that they share your core values. From time to time you should make a redefinition of your values, because your values shift and change as you evolve. You might want to discuss your values with your friends; it can be very insightful and sometimes surprising.

Saturday 24th

Venus, in a happy conversation with Saturn, makes your heart bloom. You have all the resources ready, the checklist and the building blocks and you are starting to rebuild. Saturn is on its way out of your sign and once he leaves the foundation has to hold steady for the next 30 years.

. . . .

Sunday 25th

In the darkness, there is a light. It's your inner light, and today your mind becomes acquainted with it. To comprehend it entirely, you need to allow some time. When you are in the midst of something you often can't see the woods for the trees.

Monday 26th

It could be an emotional day, more emotional than your days usually are. Your imagination can be high and you might be able to focus it outwards, but only if you work and connect with people who you know well and feel comfortable with. Avoid working on your own today, if you can; there is a tendency for daydreaming.

Tuesday 27th

Do you have high hopes regarding your immediate environment? Are you feeling super comfortable? Is it possible you idealise your circumstances or the comforts they offer? Meditate on this and see if everything really is the way you like it, or if it's just a habit you have learned to love.

Wednesday 28th

While still in retrograde, Mercury comes back to Libra as if he had forgotten to check on something. Venus is also entering Libra, so there is another emphasis on this area. You want to be appreciated in your career and vocational path. What aspect of your public image do you want to re-evaluate?

. . . .

Thursday 29th

Your emotional focus is on home and family matters and
you are willing to take action. You may feel a strong need for
a work-life balance, and yet the demands are sometimes so
conflicting that you don't know how to reconcile them. It will
take a little longer to work out the solution. Have patience.

Friday 30th

Today is another opportunity to solve conflicts with your family,
while simultaneously learning to stand up for yourself and not
banging your head against a wall. If you can release more of
the beliefs stemming from your childhood, it will become more
comfortable and allow more healing to take place.

Saturday 31st

A productive spark is waiting to burst out on today's Blue
Moon and another side of you is likely to be revealed.
Instead of keeping it subdued or locked away in favour of
practicalities, as usual, let your mind and imagination have
free reign. You'll be surprised at what you can create.

NOVEMBER

. . . .

Sunday 1st

You want to spend this day in companionship and dedicate it to joy, passion and self-expression. Sudden opportunities wish to be embraced, so you need some flexibility to make the most out of it. There can be a tendency to over-indulge, but snacking in moderation is advised.

Monday 2nd

Monday morning and your full hands-on mentality is asked for. You are in your element, focused on the mountaintop and setting one foot in front of the other. Your determination makes others go green with envy, which you might not even notice. Everything is in order, so keep it going.

Tuesday 3rd

You're busy with all sorts of chores, meetings and calls, and it might feel as if there's no time to take a break. It's one of those days when you know you have to take a small time out somewhere: stand upright, feet on the ground and breathe deeply and consciously. Now off you go again.

Wednesday 4th

Good times: Mercury retrograde is over! What you're aiming to learn from this is likely for you to be more explicit. You want to set high standards and, over the coming weeks, you will find the right people to support you on your future endeavours.

Thursday 5th

Don't forget to invest time in your one-on-one relationships.
When you focus too much on public demands, you can easily
neglect the important people in your life. You might get an
idea from a business partner to truly practise equality and
fairness in your career path and become a role model.

Friday 6th

When you take action, you need to stand by your integrity
and be true to who you are. To feel emotionally safe, you need
to find your own way of doing things. You might come to a
crossroads today and decide which way to go. Go with Frankie
and sing: I did it my way.

Saturday 7th

Take another hard look at your resources and the financial
support that can come to you when you dare to show your
full colours. Multiple resources are available, the question is:
are you willing to truly be yourself? You need to love yourself
wholeheartedly in all aspects to make this possible.

Sunday 8th

There is tension around your ability to shine because there
are still things you want to hide away. Have a think about your
shadow side, because often it is not only about integrating our
darker parts, but discovering what light you are hiding out of
your own fear to shine.

Monday 9th

As the Moon is coming back to your area of education and vision, you are asked to focus on the essence of your true desires. If you are true to yourself and allow some sense of personal utopia, what comes to mind? You can take practical steps towards this as nobody but you knows how to make it reality.

Tuesday 10th

Mercury is about to leave the area of vocation and career, and comes back to find your tribe and those who can support you on your journey. You now know what legacy you are aiming for and you know who is needed by your side. Your inner detective is back in the game.

Wednesday 11th

A fantastic day to plan, structure and move ahead first and foremost regarding your vision and dreams, and later today also regarding your legacy, which goes hand in hand anyway. You can feel how things are moving forward even, if it is all at a slow pace; it's not a race, is it?

Thursday 12th

It's the final meeting of Jupiter and Pluto. You have worked hard on yourself to integrate all aspects of your character, and become who you need to be to grow beyond your old limits. Transformation is an ongoing process, and if you focus on your core values, you will always be able to evolve beyond your expectations.

Friday 13th

The energy is getting lower, the days are now darker, and to brighten it up you might need the company of your friends. So once work is done, have a meet up, sit comfortably and have some tea and deep conversations. Chances are that you'll find comfort and some profound truth.

Saturday 14th

Mars retrograde is over. It gave a hard look at your ego, your inner child and the way you stand up for yourself. Your family and your home will still remain in focus but you are now able to do things right, and to investigate what did not work out before, now that you've changed your perspective.

Sunday 15th

The New Moon in Scorpio is a deep and reflective one. You might think it asks you to be on your own, but you can investigate and reflect better while in conversation with the people you want to connect to. Finding your tribe should be high on your list.

Monday 16th

So many right questions, opinions and thoughts, your head is still swirling with all the information received. To process, you might draw back and seek comfort in nature. With Venus and Jupiter in a discussion, are you conscious what blessings you receive from the outside world? Practise gratitude.

Tuesday 17th

An old belief stored inside of yourself could be that you are not worthy of having fun and need to stick to your responsibilities at all costs. What if you can combine it? Accountability is excellent, and you will be even better if you reserve a spot for joy.

Wednesday 18th

Act from integrity and you're able to resolve a conflict regarding home and family quickly. This conflict can raise an important question: what action is needed to find the right tribe? Remind yourself what you need to feel emotionally safe. That is the key.

Thursday 19th

Combining your deepest desires with Saturnian determination is a formula of success. You might want to do exactly that today, and set another essential building block on your path to mastery. You should feel self-confident and deeply connected to your inner core. Somebody is standing loyally by your side, supporting every step you take.

Friday 20th

It's a question of self-worth that determines how much you dare to express yourself. You could be irritated if you receive extensive positive feedback by doing something that you see as rebellious. Chances are that your parts, often considered quirky, are not so quirky at all or are at least very welcome.

Saturday 21st

There are two fundamental shifts at once. Venus is entering Scorpio to make sure you set the right boundaries in the relationship with your tribe and friends, while the Sun enters Sagittarius and you will find yourself focusing more on your inside and retreat from the outside world. Being in nature is especially important.

Sunday 22nd

With the Moon in Pisces, you're likely to enjoy the comfort of your neighbourhood and strolling around near local rivers or lakes. Take some time to listen to water, maybe take a hot coffee or tea with you. Once you're back, allow some time for daydreaming and have your notebook handy to write down your thoughts.

Monday 23rd

The Moon is crossing Neptune, so imagination and dreams are vivid. Messages from your subconscious can arise, and you should delay any important meetings if you have them. You've worked really hard in the last month. Aim to find ways to reduce your working time or go on annual leave during the next few weeks.

Tuesday 24th

The need for reflection and embracing the spirit world is still high. Try to stay at home or leave work early. Starting later would be another option. You might want to dive into a book or a movie to explore a different sense of reality. Messages can hide in a movie, too.

Wednesday 25th

You might be a little impatient today, and there's an urge to take action. Most likely, your efforts will relate to your home and family. It's an opportunity to redecorate, rearrange and create a magical atmosphere. Allow some magic to enter your life and feel your inner child jumping with joy.

Thursday 26th

Find ways to really nurture your inner child. Yes, you are grown-up, and yes, you have responsibilities and duties, but a happy child creates a happy adult. There is lots of power in freeing your inner child and meeting its needs no matter what. Have cocoa, jump around or listen to an audiobook.

Friday 27th

Stick with the inner child and think about what you enjoyed most when you were little. What was fun and had you focused for hours? Try and integrate at least one of these activities back into your life. Mercury and Pluto unlock a treasure, and you recognise how much you have transformed.

Saturday 28th

Imagination still runs high, and you want to keep on embracing joyfulness. The Sun in Sagittarius sparks you with optimism and the time you spend reflecting on yourself is well worth it. Life is beautiful, and you should get ready to create new beliefs about its meaning.

Sunday 29th

This seems to be a golden week for you, especially if you're allowed to really focus on yourself. You receive new insights from a talk with a friend and feel connected to universal truth. You may get excited about the future and should perhaps enjoy having an extra special dinner tonight, just to celebrate life.

Monday 30th

The month ends with the Gemini Full Moon and a partial lunar eclipse. They say eclipses are fated times, and this one asks you to focus on your everyday life. What do you like about it and what do you want it to become? Changes lie ahead, but it's up to you to choose the direction.

DECEMBER

. . . .

Tuesday 1st

Are your ready for the finalé of 2020? This is no usual holiday season – it's going to be an intense month with chapters closing and a massive shift ahead. With the Moon crossing the north node, you'll feel the future. As Mercury comes into Sagittarius, you might want to write a diary.

Wednesday 2nd

Did you make your first diary entry? It is a fantastic tool and will assist you in your thoughtful work, and that will set you up for your future big time. Today, you want to enjoy togetherness; nurture and support your partner or a close friend.

Thursday 3rd

Remind yourself that giving and taking should be balanced and that your needs, as well as your partner's ones, count. Instead of compromises, create win-win situations that feel nurturing for both of you. Express your feelings and allow yourself to be vulnerable. This needs trust, but provides for a more profound encounter.

Friday 4th

Some questions you can ponder and write in your diary today are: how do you want to shine? How do you want to show up and where are you playing a role that isn't entirely authentic? Lots of questions, but the answers will help to set you up for the future.

Saturday 5th

Your self-expression is linked to the role you see yourself in, and if you get clear about that, you suddenly have a new range of options available. This might also be related to your inner child and how much reassurance you received when you were little.

Sunday 6th

Are you ready for a dreamy Sunday? Your dream could be very vivid as Venus is connecting to Neptune. It is also a day to embrace love. The compassionate, selfless love for the planet, animals and humankind itself. Earthly love. What is your vision of love?

Monday 7th

Do you have a vision board? It's an excellent time to start one. All you need is a piece of paper, pencils and maybe some photos. Start to picture your wishes and desires in a way that you can express them most naturally. If you do it digitally, make a print to make it more tangible.

Tuesday 8th

It's a fantastic day to make plans, renew your to-do lists and be pragmatic about the work you do. You are able to focus on work and get things organised. If you need to prepare stuff for Christmas, it's an excellent opportunity to line things up early.

Wednesday 9th

Be aware, not everything is the way it seems. Aim to be extremely honest, especially to yourself. The chances are that a truth revealed can make you feel uncomfortable, but not speaking or recognising it would set you out on the wrong path. It may be a blessing in disguise.

Thursday 10th

Sometimes, it's better to be safe than sorry. With Venus in Scorpio connecting to Pluto, you're extremely capable of setting the necessary boundaries and installing a sense of security. Still, something in your perception can be off. Just turn yourself upside down, metaphorically, to see another perspective and have an 'aha' moment.

Friday 11th

Say goodbye to old beliefs, today. Take some time for yourself and note down all the beliefs you came across throughout this year. Look especially at those related to your inner child and your parents. Release those that no longer serve you in peace with a little ritual.

Saturday 12th

The Moon and Venus join together, and you might be able to see them in the morning sky. Meet some friends today and enjoy their company. Other than that, it's a day to set the course for the future. If you want to start a new habit as part of your daily routine, now is a really good time to start.

Sunday 13th

This Sunday should be a good one for you. Get outside in nature and have a wander, maybe walking through the snow and tuning into universal truth while you explore your inner world. Make it a sacred day, dedicated to you. It isn't a day to get stuff done. If there are things to do, delay them until at least Tuesday if you can.

Monday 14th

Happy New Moon in Sagittarius. This one is likely to have a feeling of melancholy attached to it. The old is almost done, new shifts are about to happen, and there is another call to release old and outdated beliefs and replace them with new ones. Life has far more in store for you.

Tuesday 15th

If you have things left on your to-do list, roll up your sleeves and get the job done. If you're in charge, you could also aid others in moving forward with a structure and create very concrete results. The only downside to this energy can be that you might be unstoppable and work on and on.

Wednesday 16th

This is the final time that the Moon finds so many planetary bodies in your sign. You might almost literally feel the vibration of the change ahead. Take a look in the mirror today and acknowledge yourself for all the changes you've been through, for never giving up and moving on relentlessly.

. . . .

Thursday 17th

Mark your calendar. There is a huge announcement to make: Saturn is leaving your sign and enters into Aquarius. Your future starts today. It's now all about your self-worth, a new approach to your possessions and your values. It is grounding the vision and creating a new reality.

Friday 18th

Mercury is in the heart of the Sun to receive a message of great importance. As always, allow some time for it to sink in. It's a message about your beliefs and how you want to integrate spirituality in your daily life. Meanwhile, you thrive on the feeling of revolution.

Saturday 19th

Jupiter has his final day in your sign. He enjoyed guiding you, but there was a lot to face. In the upcoming year, Jupiter will help you anchor in the new with more optimism and enthusiasm. Make today a day of gratitude for all the blessings you have received in 2020.

Sunday 20th

Just as Jupiter enters Aquarius, it runs into Saturn waiting at the doorstep. When these two meet, there is a new cycle starting. They want to agree on the terms of building a new world and reality. You have probably set everything up straight and are ready to go. How exciting!

Monday 21st

Happy Winter Solstice. Everything is going quickly, so here is the next major event: a turning of the tides. This marks the shortest day, longest night and the light returning. Be on the lookout for new opportunities on this, the beginning of your birthday season.

Tuesday 22nd

What is your favourite thing about Christmas? What is your inner child's favourite thing? Make sure that you include some of the traditions you love in this year's celebration. If there are last-minute changes to be made, take care of them as soon as possible.

Wednesday 23rd

Today can indicate power struggles, maybe regarding the preparations for this season's celebrations. The key is to maintain integrity, speak your truth, but do everything you can to find a solution. You might need to agree to disagree and stay busy throughout the day, so that you have an outlet for all the energy available to you.

Thursday 24th

What a blessing that Moon enters in the sign of Taurus to ensure a peaceful celebration. You should find yourself able to make the final arrangements and have a relaxed evening. Let joy be your anchor point for this year's Christmas celebration and if there are kids involved, focus your attention on them.

Friday 25th

Merry Christmas! You might find an astonishing gift today that supports your self-expression. Other than that, make sure that you thoroughly enjoy the day, the board games, running around with the children and eating mince pies and pudding. Feel the joy and spread the love!

Saturday 26th

Your dreams are never far away. You still feel like you could sing all the time and today asks you to connect to your imagination. You might want to sit somewhere cosy, perhaps getting snug with the family and reading tales, telling your own stories or diving into some movies.

Sunday 27th

Today can feel busy, even though it's a Sunday and one could think it is about resting. Not for you, as you want to feel a sense of routine, getting lots of chores done, and keeping up your new habits. No need to wait for the New Year to start; the time is now.

Monday 28th

The energy is high, the Sun connects to Uranus, and together they set the revolutionising energy free. It's this sense of newness you are happy to create and integrate into your new everyday routine. A considerable part of this new routine is consciously taking breaks and spending some time in nature to recharge.

Tuesday 29th

Today marks a Full Moon in Cancer, illuminating your relationships. There was a similar Full Moon at the beginning of the year. See if you can look back now and explore how much has changed and how much you could improve your love life by focusing on nurturing yourself.

Wednesday 30th

What is love? Is it Earthly love, divine love and universal love? Take your sweetheart by the hand and go for a walk under the starry sky. Let your imagination guide you through the universe and make some wishes. Where do you see your path unfolding together?

Thursday 31st

New Year's Eve is here; 2020 was an intense ride with major cycles coming to a close and new ones that are just beginning. The road ahead is exciting and will feel much lighter. The world needs you and your skills to anchor in the new world. Lead by example.

Capricorn

....

DAILY FORECASTS
for 2021

JANUARY

Friday 1st

Happy New Year and welcome to 2021. The year begins on the back of a Full Moon in your relationship sector. You may find that a new level of understanding has been achieved, and you are able to communicate your dreams and intentions for the year with greater clarity. Take some time today to reflect on what has been and what you want to come.

Saturday 2nd

Saying what you feel and meaning what you say will be received well by others. You may find that your divine purpose this year is to lead from the heart and release some restrictions you place on yourself. Finish up any family matters in the next few days while Mars is lending you the energy to do so.

Sunday 3rd

The Moon slips into your travel sector today. You may be double-checking future plans or systematically working through your planner for the year. Schedule in some time for doing things that are unusual and may bring out your creative side. Think outside the box for innovative travel or higher education ideas.

Monday 4th

Communication with long and short distance contacts is highlighted today. You may prefer to concentrate on things further afield, but short-term dreams need your attention too. Your close friends may be your soul group, so listen to them for advice and direction. These will be more important to you in the long run.

Tuesday 5th

Mercury meets Pluto today in your own sign. This heralds a time where you must be aware of messages and signposts that show you the next steps on your life path. Pluto asks for permanent change and Mercury will tell you how to make this happen. Keep your eyes, ears and mind open for possibilities.

Wednesday 6th

Mars spends his final day in your family sector. You may have to rally the troops and initiate something beneficial to your tribe. It's possible that this has already been planned and you now have the green light to forge ahead. You're active and productive today. Don't be too forceful.

Thursday 7th

Achieving harmony in the workplace may be tricky today, as your heart is just not in it. You may be focused on making fresh starts and forgetting that there is outstanding or ongoing work to be done. Mars moves into your creative sector and your senses may start tingling with new ideas.

Friday 8th

You may have a moment of crisis this morning, or even a sleepless night. You have a lot on your mind and can't fix your thoughts. This can be unsettling but will soon pass. Your wider social groups are calling for you to engage in deep philosophical discussion this weekend.

. . . .

Saturday 9th

Venus, the planet of love and harmony, enters your sign.
She will bring beauty and fun to into areas where you are
sometimes too strict with yourself. Mercury also shifts signs
and becomes the trader in your finance and value sector.
If you have business transactions to make, this should be a
promising time.

Sunday 10th

If you look carefully, you may get a glimpse of the next step
of your personal growth. The Sun connects to Neptune and
burns away any disillusions you have been under. You may
also hear from a wise teacher or leader who has an important
lesson for you.

Monday 11th

The Moon in your hidden sector may be keeping you awake with
wild dreams and fantasies. You may be reaching out or planning
to see the wider world. Mercury bumps into Jupiter and this
influence can make your thoughts even bigger. You may feel
unstoppable now, but make sure that you play by the rules.

Tuesday 12th

Mercury and Uranus are squaring off. It's possible that you
have a dispute over money and resources today. Uranus tends
to disrupt the status quo, so you may need to check that your
bank balance is supporting your dreams. This energy may also
be wildly creative or even lead to romantic overtures; try to
harness it and use it positively.

Wednesday 13th

Today there's a New Moon in your sign. This is a great chance to make goals and intentions that are all about you and your self-improvement. However, you must make sure that plans are realistically achievable, as reaching too high or aspiring beyond your capabilities will only lead to a fall.

Thursday 14th

The Sun meets Pluto in your sign. You may see a battle of egos or power struggles. Alternatively, you may now understand what it is that is going to change permanently. Seek advice and get informed, as there are people around who can pass on their knowledge today.

Friday 15th

Today may be quiet but you have much to think about. You desire to be part of the collective and do your bit for the community. You may even have ideas of joining a good cause. Stay with your emotions today and go where they lead, and you may be pleasantly surprised.

Saturday 16th

Merging with your closest friends and relatives will be a good activity for the weekend. Your mind may be drawn towards spiritual groups or learning about mystical concepts. You may be more sensitive than usual and wish to connect with people you haven't heard from in some time.

Sunday 17th

Today you may be extra dreamy to the point of being unrealistic. The Moon has met Neptune and you may be drifting away to fantasy land. If you can keep one foot on the ground, you will get some insight into what it is like to surrender control and go with the flow.

Monday 18th

Jupiter and Uranus are challenging you to look at finances and how much support you have for new creative projects. You may need to bend the rules today. You feel energised and may wish to lead in family matters. If you don't abuse the privilege then your leadership should be welcomed.

Tuesday 19th

The Sun moves into your finance and value sector. You will now be able to get a good look at what you think is worth your time and effort. Your own self-worth is involved here too. Ensure that you gain from anything you invest in, or you will experience negative feelings further down the line.

Wednesday 20th

Mars meets Uranus today in your creative sector. This is highly volatile energy, but not all bad. You will notice how your personal energy picks up and you may have creative projects filling you up and ready to go. Instability can be inspirational, too. Great ideas may now be formed. It's time to explore your imagination.

· · · · · · · · · · · · · · · · · ·

Thursday 21st

Today that high energy is ongoing, and you may find that you are emotionally invested now as the Moon sits with Mars and Uranus. This may lead to rows and disputes. It's likely that you experience conflict with elders or bosses. Keep the peace by keeping out of unnecessary dramas.

Friday 22nd

You may find that today is much quieter, and any negative atmospheres have dissipated. You may be in the mood for love, comfort foods or simply a good time with good company. Be careful not to talk about finances or things you feel strongly about with the wrong people, as it has the possibility of turning the day upside down.

Saturday 23rd

This afternoon may be a day of simply getting all the chores done and doing your duty. You may be undecided about how you wish to spend your free time and could be easily coaxed into doing another's bidding. The potential is there for you to put yourself first if you wish.

Sunday 24th

The Moon passes the point of fate in your health and duties sector. You may be wondering what more is out there for you. As the Moon sits with your ruler, Saturn, you feel that you have too many responsibilities and your dreams are just castles in the sky.

Monday 25th

Mars and Jupiter are making a connection which you may find challenging in your financial and creative sectors. There may be a tendency to overindulge or spend too much today. This evening, you may wish to spend quality time with a lover or to treat yourself to some self-care.

Tuesday 26th

Today, you may bring out your soft, sensitive side. It may feel nice to be protected by a lover or you may be nurturing someone else. It's possible that you feel some agitation and you are the one needing to be spoon-fed and comforted. Ice cream and movies should satisfy this need.

Wednesday 27th

The planets in your sign are opposing the Moon today and making things tense. You may feel that if you allow yourself to be soft, then you are relinquishing control. This is not true. You're as powerful as ever, but you are allowed some downtime too. Listen to you own needs and look after yourself.

Thursday 28th

You rise again under a fearless Full Moon in your intimacy sector. Many planetary connections are just waiting for you to crash and burn, and this may feel tough. Stand up for yourself and don't be afraid to show deep feelings. You have a voice; use it well, today.

Friday 29th

The Sun meets Jupiter, today. This can be a highly beneficial time, full of positive and optimistic energy. This happens in your finances and value sector, which indicates that you may have a windfall if you're lucky. All money matters are favoured. You may also see a clash of big egos or an exposure of truth.

Saturday 30th

Mercury turns retrograde tomorrow in your sign. Use today to make all the necessary preparations. Back up all your technical devices and double-check travel plans. Take extra care on the roads and be mindful of how you communicate. Take everything slower until this event is over.

Sunday 31st

Mercury retrograde begins. You will need to retrace your steps from the last three weeks and reconsider your affirmations to yourself. Look at how realistic they are. Have you overstretched and put an unachievable goal in your path? Make plans for smaller steps and smaller goals, and you won't go far wrong.

FEBRUARY

. . . .

Monday 1st

Venus spends her final day in your sign. She will now help
to bring in some finances and let you see more value in the
wider world and organisations. This afternoon, you're likely
to be more focused on achieving balance and fair play in the
workplace. Be careful not to be too aggressively outspoken.

Tuesday 2nd

Conflict may erupt and finances will need an overhaul today.
This will be a personal matter and can be unsettling, but other
aspects favour good fortune in the workplace. You may have
said your piece and those in charge have noted it. You may
even receive an apology from someone.

Wednesday 3rd

The Moon connects to Mercury retrograde and you may feel
the effects of this in the workplace. Be mindful and practise the
pause before responding. You may have to bite your tongue.
Relationships between men and women can be difficult today.
Assertiveness may become bullying behaviour. You, however,
can stay in control today.

Thursday 4th

Today has very tricky energy to navigate. An intense Moon in
your social sector causes a rumble in many areas. It may be
tough to express yourself within groups, and you may get on
the wrong side of a leader or important person. Use your good
communication skills to settle things.

Friday 5th

Jealousy and nastiness may surface within your wider groups today. You may be the target of gossip, or even be the one spreading it. There will be a bitter aftertaste at the end of the day, and you may have to agree to disagree. A valuable lesson may be learned here.

Saturday 6th

Venus meets Saturn today in your finances and value sector. This can feel like someone is restricting your flow or making sure that you look at all the facts before making a silly mistake. You may need to tighten the purse strings and go without a little luxury.

Sunday 7th

Venus is squaring off with Uranus. There may possibly be tantrums or acting out and you may not be sensitive to the needs of others, especially if there's childish and selfish behaviour going on. You may be annoyed that this has distracted you from some precious time to yourself.

Monday 8th

The Moon dips into your sign and helps you to get active and inventive. You may have many projects ready and waiting to flourish, and today you should put some of your heart back into making them grow. Mercury is in the heart of the Sun and asks you to listen to dreams and messages.

Tuesday 9th

Today there's great energy available for you to make small changes and set about putting short-term plans in place. You may have found a different perspective, and this should help you to transform projects that were going nowhere into real possibilities. Stay in control of this.

Wednesday 10th

This is a day where you may feel upside down or inside out. The Moon passes over all the planets in your finances and value sector. Conflicting emotions surface fleetingly but soon pass. You may feel very tired by the end of the day. Don't commit to anything right now.

Thursday 11th

A New Moon in your finances and values sector meets Mercury retrograde. Today is your chance to try to view something objectively and make an action plan. You may not have much energy, but this is fine. Don't act yet. You may wish to do some spiritual practice, as this will help.

Friday 12th

The Moon drops into your communications sector, making you desire to merge with the collective or with spirit. You may feel as if you're waiting for a green light to get active again. Rest for now as this will come. Make sure you have all you need.

Saturday 13th

The dreamy Moon meets Neptune and this connection helps you to get back on track. Neptune can show you where your true north is and acts as your inner compass. You may feel more aligned today, and desire to connect with people you love via email, messages or a visit.

Sunday 14th

Most of the day you may be romantic, idealistic and feeling blissful. If you can manage to stay connected to Earth too, you may find something out that gives you some advantage. However, Mercury retrograde meets Jupiter and mishaps or misunderstandings may be more or bigger today. Be careful out there.

Monday 15th

Today you have more energy and are getting out and about, implementing and planning with family. Your leadership skills are tested by both Jupiter and Saturn. How far are you willing to go? How strict can you be? Remember personal boundaries and joy will come easily.

Tuesday 16th

Notice how today you have a more nurturing outlook to those in your charge. Venus connects to the energetic Moon and reminds you that groups work best if there is compassion and empathy between them. A little love and encouragement will go a long way today, so extend your hands to someone.

Wednesday 17th

The Moon enters your creative sector and meets Uranus. You may have some bright ideas on how to solve a long-standing problem today. It's possible that you are needed to be grounded and focused within a group. You have a solid, ambitious nature, which others will benefit from.

Thursday 18th

The Sun enters your communications sector for a month. Your conversations and spiritual life will have more life and clarity now. You may be driven and slightly bossy today. Someone may not be pulling their weight and you find that you are irritated by this. You may be impatient with them.

Friday 19th

Venus and Mars are squaring off today. This energy highlights your annoyance with others who aren't acting correctly within a group. You must take control of this situation and teach others your skills of taking one step at a time in order to achieve success in all that you do.

Saturday 20th

The weekend is here, and you may simply be seeing to mundane jobs and getting things done. However, you may not do a very good job of it as the chances are that you'll be feeling unfocused. Ask for help and co-create with someone. Exchanging ideas whilst working can help you in the future.

Sunday 21st

Mercury turns direct today. You may now have more insight and clarity on how to continue your self-development. As the Moon meets the point of fate, it's likely that you have seen your destination as a faraway place. Take the first step towards it today; a journey must begin somewhere, after all.

Monday 22nd

This morning, you feel more inclined to nurture yourself and someone close to you. You desire to feel safe and secure and will seek out people who are softer than you. It may be that you wish to spend time in the company of intuitive women. Connect with mother figures now.

Tuesday 23rd

A gentle Moon connects to Neptune, who is guiding you in the right direction. You may feel the need to connect with spiritual people or with those you regard as your tribe. Take care that this watery energy doesn't overwhelm you, as you may then feel unsafe or bogged down.

Wednesday 24th

Today the Moon opposes Pluto and you may have a moment where you lack self-control. This can be a trigger, asking you to end or transform something, and you may feel defensive and protective. This afternoon you should find your voice and courage. Deeper mysteries are awaiting your discovery.

Thursday 25th

You may well get on the wrong side of everyone today as you have unstable emotions that are changeable and conflicted. It could be that you're coming over as a narcissistic know-it-all. Venus swims into your communications sector, where she will be ethereal and share her love around.

Friday 26th

As the weekend arrives, you may be planning or scheduling a trip. Connecting with people overseas is possible too. Use the weekend to declutter your inbox and make space for new information. You may find that you are reluctant to join group ventures now and prefer to be alone.

Saturday 27th

A Full Moon in your travel sector throws the spotlight on the last six months of achievement here. What might have come to fruition now? Look closely and you may see that some details have been left out, which you must rectify. A health problem may come to light at this time.

Sunday 28th

Planets in earth signs make you feel stable and grounded today. You can take respite in the fact that you always do your best and strive to get to the top. It's possible that you are at the summit now and looking down on your efforts. Reward yourself.

MARCH

. . . .

Monday 1st

Today you are fair-minded and do your best to communicate effectively with those in the workplace. You may find that you are negotiating deals regarding finances. People will notice how professional you are now, so put your best foot forward and make responsible proposals. This is a lucky day.

Tuesday 2nd

A balanced approach to your work is not only advisable but also necessary. You will not have a problem with this as you prefer to get to the top with the least amount of effort and the most amount of prestige. You should find yourself working well with others today.

Wednesday 3rd

The Moon enters your social sector and it's possible that you discover intrigue or come across something distasteful. Uranus is facing the Moon here and disrupts the harmony between friends and wider groups. This is something to investigate, as it may have underlying reasons which are justifiable.

Thursday 4th

You have understanding for anyone who may be suffering right now and can see both sides of a heated discussion. Big issues that concern the collective and your role in it are under the microscope. Mars enters your health and duties sector. You may have a period of being energised or, conversely, feeling burnt out.

Friday 5th

The Moon and Mars face off and you may already be feeling very tired. Time alone is advised as debates between friends and interest groups can get heated. Remember to honour your personal boundaries and keep yourself safe. It isn't your job to agree with everyone and keep the peace.

Saturday 6th

The Moon connects to Mercury and Jupiter today. This will influence your private thoughts and emotions. It could be that you are trying to get to the bottom of something. It's possible that a new idea or concept can be grasped if you give it enough thought without distractions.

Sunday 7th

Today you are rested and back in good form. The Moon is back in your sign, but you may feel a little self-indulgent and take care of your own needs without thinking of others. Uranus and Venus connect, and their influence can mean that you take what you want today.

Monday 8th

You are in touch with your inner compass today and begin to feel your way back into your groups. This is a great time to reconnect with the collective whilst keeping your personal dreams and visions in sight. There's much work to be done and you're ready for it.

Tuesday 9th

When Pluto hosts the Moon's monthly visit, your self-control is strong – sometimes too strong – and you deny yourself rest and pleasure. Check-in with your health today, as your energy to do your daily duties is leaving you no free time to unwind in the evening.

Wednesday 10th

The Sun meets Neptune today and it's now glaringly obvious what your inner compass is pointing to. All of Neptune's mists have been burned away and you may see something that you have previously overlooked. You may feel a push-and-pull type of energy in your heart until you have re-calibrated yourself.

Thursday 11th

Your mind may be very busy today. Headaches are likely, unless you find a way to concentrate on one thing at a time. You may already be feeling burnt out by Mars in your health and duties sector. Use his energy to begin a new health regime and pay more attention to your health.

Friday 12th

This is a good day for artistic and creative projects as you get new ideas or are able to solve a problem. Conversations with others may seem vague and unrealistic but can be food for thought for something bold. Words of love may be expressed now.

Saturday 13th

A New Moon in your communications sector meets Neptune. This is a great opportunity to promise yourself a new beginning or to embark on a vision quest. Religion, spiritual retreats or solo projects – especially on your self-growth – can be off to a good start if you start now under this New Moon.

Sunday 14th

Venus meets Neptune and adds beauty and harmony to your goals and intentions. These may appear to be surreal and unattainable but stick with it, it will do you good to embrace your emotional side. Be constructive and make solid plans. Create a mind map of the steps to take.

Monday 15th

You have great energy today and can organise fun activities within your family groups. Initiating a get-together for today or in the future is right up your street. Make the necessary contacts and get the ball rolling. Others will follow your lead and absorb your enthusiasm.

Tuesday 16th

Mercury has entered your communications sector. This is great news. You will see an increase in the volume of messaging, research, teaching and learning now. Expect to be initiated into spiritual groups or find your own path by networking with others. Enjoy sensual delights today, such as good food and company.

Wednesday 17th

The Moon meets Uranus in your creative sector. You may find that you have a sudden burst of artistic or romantic energy. This may be too much for some and you will need to remember personal boundaries. This isn't a day to profess undying love for someone special.

Thursday 18th

Today is much better for expressing your desires and making your feelings known. You will get a boost of romanticism from Venus and Neptune, which means that sharing your dreams with someone is possible now. Just be careful not to make grand gestures that another may not be ready for yet.

Friday 19th

The Moon is now in your health and duties sector. This may not be an easy day unless you play by the rules and remember which duties you must attend to. You may find that when the Moon meets Mars, you are emotionally drained and need time out by evening.

Saturday 20th

Today is the Spring Equinox, and days and nights are equal lengths. The Sun is now in your family sector and is ready to act on any plans you have made. You may be eager to please but irritated by slower people who have not yet committed to a family gathering.

Sunday 21st

Your energy today can vary widely. You will need to prioritise your chores and make time for your own interests. This can be difficult, and you may find at the end of the day that you have achieved very little. Venus moves into your family sector to harmonise the troops.

Monday 22nd

Important relationships need your attention today. The Moon sits in your opposite sign and you relate to those who appear to look after you well. Mercury and Uranus are making a great connection, which helps you to speak from your heart and connect to interesting people.

Tuesday 23rd

Enjoy the emotional, dreamy energy of today with a loved one or friend you admire. Your inner compass is pointing north today and showing you that some things are best left behind for good. Pluto sits opposite, receiving any garbage you wish to dispose of now. What doesn't nurture you can be released.

Wednesday 24th

Venus is in the heart of the Sun today. She is glowing with love which will rain down on your family sector. This may be a day to support a family member who is struggling. You may find that you're doing extra chores, but these will ultimately benefit your family group.

Thursday 25th

You may still be feeling the tremendous, uplifting energy in your family sector. A new level of relating and encouraging has been reached. A fiery Moon in your intimacy sector enhances this with love and compassion for all. Be true to yourself and lead from the heart.

Friday 26th

The Moon drops into your travel sector. Check-in with your health now and how you are of service to others. This is a time where you check details and facts and become interested in travel with a purpose. Other cultures will fascinate you and a new journey beckons.

Saturday 27th

Today can be tricky as your energy will fluctuate. You could have lost sight of your own dreams and may not be communicating or understanding a new concept well. Take a step back and look at things objectively. What needs to be tweaked in order for today to work for you?

Sunday 28th

A Full Moon lights up your career sector. You may notice that something has finally come to completion. It's possible that you also have new insight or have solved a problem. Venus opposes the Moon and asks that you consider your personal role along with that of the group at work.

Monday 29th

The week begins with excellent energy for you to access.
You have the right amount of energy to work with others
and achieve much. This may be rewarded at a later date as
finances are highlighted. You may also see a rise in your
status as your work might be commended.

Tuesday 30th

If you need to be ruthless today then this is possible, although
you may have to upset some people. Speak your mind if you
must but be aware that you may come across as slightly deluded.
Mercury sits with Neptune today and talks all sorts of nonsense.

Wednesday 31st

Are you in the mood for a midweek social event? This could
simply be interacting with your online interest groups
and getting things off your chest. You may have some wild
interests and wish to discuss things. Find the right people who
will encourage and support you in this.

APRIL

. . . .

Thursday 1st

Today your thoughts turn inwards and you may be fantasising about places to go and courses to study. Your hidden sector is where you process thoughts and feelings which you don't want exposed. You may be secretly yearning to be free and rebellious, but your sensible self always keeps you grounded. Look for compromise here.

Friday 2nd

Mercury and Pluto are having a talk. You will get a better idea of the changes you need to make, and this may mean that you reinvent yourself several times over. If you're reliable and get your daily tasks done, is it really a problem for you or others?

Saturday 3rd

How do you talk to yourself? Today, your heart isn't willing to listen to Mercury, who represents your mind. He wants you to take action somehow. Maybe a holiday or a new line of study is just what you need. Less work and more play for you.

Sunday 4th

The Moon is in your sign now and you are more self-assured. However, be warned that what you are feeling may be a kind of self-avoidance as you don't allow yourself much freedom. Enjoy some sensual delights such as good food and let your hair down a little today.

Monday 5th

Mercury has shifted into your family sector. He will urge you to start new things, so stop procrastinating. The Moon meets Pluto in your sign and you may feel that familiar niggling that something has to go or be transformed forever. Little steps will suffice for now.

Tuesday 6th

Venus and Mars are making a helpful connection today and you may wish to use this energy in your close relationships. An outgoing mood will help you to reach out to others and combine work with pleasure. Males and female energies will work well together today. They may even come up with something innovative.

Wednesday 7th

The Moon in your finances and value sector makes relating to others easier today. Everyone may be cooperating with each other and working towards a common goal. Jupiter adds optimism and joy now and you may find yourself involved in a good cause. Do what makes you happy.

Thursday 8th

Today you may need to stop or pause what you are doing. Reflecting on how you communicate with others and are part of a team may cause you concern. This is unnecessary. You are highly valued and need to start believing that. A friend may surprise you by verifying this statement.

Friday 9th

When the Moon meets Neptune, you may see your true north once more. It may feel like it is drifting away from you. Don't be too desperate to cling onto it, as it will always be there for you. Mars is getting hot and bothered and needs you to act now.

Saturday 10th

Venus and Jupiter combine to give you a blessed day of joy, love and compassionate actions. Something may have paid off today. Victory and success are almost certain to present themselves to you. You will be seen by those in authority and rewarded for your hard work within a group.

Sunday 11th

Your mind will be very busy today. You can say what you mean and with total conviction. This will be accepted well, as you have spoken within a boundary or framework and have abided by the rules. Respect is due to you and you may well receive this today.

Monday 12th

There is a New Moon today in your family sector. This Moon meets Venus so expect any new starts to be full of love and harmony. However, Pluto has his say and reminds you to finish something up before implementing this new start, otherwise you are not likely to get very far.

Tuesday 13th

A sensual Moon in your creative sector makes you feel romantic or artistic. When the Moon meets Uranus, you may be in for a lovely surprise. You may also shock yourself by declaring words of love or by doing something unusual and out of the norm for you.

Wednesday 14th

Venus is about to leave your family sector. One last look around and you may see something that you have overlooked which needs the Venus touch now. Be guided by your dreams. Talk to someone who needs your encouragement but don't let them bring you down. Maintain healthy relating boundaries.

Thursday 15th

This morning your mood changes as there is much to do. You may be bouncing through your day and doing extra chores for others. Venus in your creative sector is about to bring more beauty and love to your artistic and romantic pursuits. This is a joyful day, so make the most of it.

Friday 16th

You may have a moment where you realise that you have done nothing for yourself recently. Change that today. Let others know that you intend to have some quality time for yourself. You will feel refreshed and able to enjoy a weekend which feeds your soul.

Saturday 17th

Mercury is the key planet today. He appears to be having a conference from your home centre and is telling those in the family and wider groups just what he thinks. This may not go down too well, as the Moon is with Mars and you may get emotional and aggressive.

Sunday 18th

Mercury is quiet now. You may find that you have spoken and silenced everyone, including yourself. Take the time to listen to those who care for and nurture you. You may need to self-protect until the fallout clears. Listen to the wise wisdom of female elders today and you may learn something valuable.

Monday 19th

The Sun and Mercury enter your creative sector together. This is great, as they will heat up your self-expression and bring much laughter. You may also find that you enjoy listening to inspiring speakers and find a muse in the next month. You may share your creative ideas more.

Tuesday 20th

Today you may be feeling a little vulnerable and retreat into the arms of someone who knows how to look after you. You may feel that you are the centre of attention in a way you dislike. Stay in your comfort zone today; this energy will soon pass.

Wednesday 21st

The Moon has shifted into your intimacy sector, but you face new challenges. An elder or boss comes into conflict with you. It's likely that your egos clash as you see things very differently. Uranus connects and adds to the rumblings of unease; be careful not to have a tantrum now.

Thursday 22nd

Mars spends his final day in your intimacy sector. You're being asked to check finances you share with another. Are they still important to you? You may wish to assert some independence and go it alone. Find another way of relating that leaves some space for personal advancement.

Friday 23rd

Venus meets Uranus and this combination can bring you a sexy, seductive time. With Mars also entering your relationship sector, you can be sure that your love life will not be boring now. Talk about the future and where you would like to go. Maybe this can be done together.

Saturday 24th

Today it may be difficult to hold on to your own dreams and visions, as you may need to see things through new eyes. It's possible that you are having deep discussions which lead to an exploration of the other. You may hear a shocking revelation or tell someone a secret.

Sunday 25th

Mercury now meets Venus and wishes to smooth things over and get back to a harmonious level. Alternatively, you may have had too much of a good thing and need to get back to normality. Your sense of duty overrides your sensual needs right now.

Monday 26th

Today you may need to relinquish control and go with the flow a little more. There may be someone in your life who can bring you what you lack. You can be too strict on yourself and then do the opposite and have a blow-out. Try to balance this today.

Tuesday 27th

Difficult energy comes with a Full Moon in your social sector. You may feel restricted in your roles within your wider groups. An opposition to Venus and Mercury can mean that you experience jealousy and nastiness. What may have come to light under this Moon? What may need an adjustment?

Wednesday 28th

Pluto turns retrograde in your sign today. You may feel like you are constantly reinventing yourself. However, the Moon in your hidden sector can give you an idea of where this next change is going to be. Look at revising your views on secrecy, jealousy, and relationships that are intense or draining.

Thursday 29th

Today you may feel the need to rest and be alone with your thoughts. You ponder the past and what achievements you have had. You may mourn or regret some things, but rest assured that they are now in the past. What skills need to be resurrected and used again now?

Friday 30th

There is highly explosive energy today as the Sun meets Uranus. This can be unstable, but you can also produce your best creative ideas to date. Get networking, make your dreams public and co-create with others. A great merging of minds and hearts can happen now.

MAY
. . . .

Saturday 1st
If there is something you need to say, express or create then today
is the perfect opportunity. You are unlikely to be hampered by
emotions which may distract you. You may make today all about
you. You may feel rebellious and refuse to conform. Stand up for
your rights and speak out.

Sunday 2nd
Today is filled with potential for you to get control and lead from
the heart. A project that is dear to you will catch your attention
and you may spend most of the day on it. Your heart is asking
for change and by evening you may have already done it.

Monday 3rd
Something or someone may get your back up. This could
come in the form of a social injustice. A valuable lesson awaits
you, regarding what you find worthy or valuable. Re-assessing
your priorities is in order as you see things through the eyes of
another or a group.

Tuesday 4th
It's likely that a good cause has awakened your feelings of
justice and you wish to help raise awareness. Mercury moves
into your health and duties sector and will help you to spread
the word in your daily, mundane work. Expect to question
everything now, however insignificant.

Wednesday 5th

You may feel more a part of your wider groups, today. Your presence and experience are appreciated. However, you may have to have stern words with a member of your group. This can be difficult but if you are mindful, you may be tactful and empathic. Great things can be achieved today.

Thursday 6th

Your personal desires and those of the collective are in sync. You may be feeling stronger and supported. There's something crucial you must attend to today, which could be legal or financial. You may be more effective than you realise, as every little effort you make certainly helps.

Friday 7th

The Moon in your communications sector connects to Pluto and Venus at either side. You may be emotionally pulled in two directions. Both of these are personal and will affect you as an individual. It's possible to blend these and make a loving change happen. Get ready for something new entering your life.

Saturday 8th

Once more you're fired up and ready for action. It may be tricky to get your family on board today and there might be a lot of unnecessary drama resulting. Not everyone is of the same mind, so your best plan of action would be to go it alone.

Sunday 9th

Venus now joins Mercury in your health and duties sector. She will help you to remember that, however you manage your day, there must always be time left for your own needs. Self-care is paramount if you are to serve others. Fill your own cup, first.

Monday 10th

A good way to self-soothe would be to shop for your favourite foods and book out some time with good company. You may wish to come back down to earth today. Your romantic partner or close friendships will provide food for thought and you may have lively discussions that help you process recent events.

Tuesday 11th

Today there is a New Moon in your creative sector. This is excellent news if you wish to begin creating, start a new romance or simply remember to enjoy the finer things in life. Look towards your dreams and factor them in if you set goals and intentions today.

Wednesday 12th

The Moon meets Venus and gives you soft, feminine energy in which you may pamper yourself or bond with women. Your intuition and sense of harmony will be high today. Research or simply gathering facts will be favoured. Organising your planner and decluttering a messy spot will also be productive activities.

Thursday 13th

You have just enough strength from the Sun in your creative sector to blow away any fog surrounding your true north. Neptune's energy helps you get back on track. The downside of this is that you may have a mind full of thoughts and a sleepless night.

Friday 14th

Jupiter is now in your communications sector. His expansive
energy can mean that you network far and wide while he's here.
You may become involved with spiritual groups and find that
your empathy and love for the collective grows. Jupiter brings
you an important twelve months ahead in this area of life.

Saturday 15th

Just as the weekend arrives, the Moon enters your relationship
sector. You may wish to enjoy some downtime with a partner
or close friend. At these times you may feel vulnerable, because
you are able to release yourself from the strict and upright
persona you wear every day.

Sunday 16th

Today is great for getting close to a partner. Mars and Uranus
connect to the Moon, making unstable but highly reactive
energy. This could mean that your partner really does rock
your world and takes you to a different level. Neptune adds his
dreamy energy to this, too.

Monday 17th

You may have had enough nurturing for now and wish to get
on with your own things. This could cause a struggle at first,
as you may be seen to be rejecting another. Your sense of duty
and responsibility to your own projects must now come first.
You're likely going to find it tough to detach.

Tuesday 18th

Today, your courage and boldness to speak about tricky or taboo subjects may be questioned by someone in authority. You will need to remember your own boundaries and not push another's too far. If you let Venus help, you can express yourself with compassion and smooth things over.

Wednesday 19th

Whatever your emotions are today, you may find that they get bigger than they need to be. Take time out and step back. Your mind and mouth may be doing overtime and you may not realise it. Others may perceive you as bossy or too outspoken for your own good.

Thursday 20th

The Sun enters your health and duties sector for the next month. This is a good time for looking after your own body, taking care that you are getting enough rest and the right foods. Use some of your time today to look at what you can clean up.

Friday 21st

You may notice that you have lost your inner guide again, but this is OK as it gives you time to concentrate on other matters such as education, travel or health. You may be more methodical and realistic, and tweak your dreams and vision for a more sensible outcome.

Saturday 22nd

Today you may be a weekend worker. There's a need for you to restore balance or harmony in the workplace, and this could mean working overtime or taking your tasks home. You may have to decline invitations or put off smaller weekend chores.

Sunday 23rd

Saturn turns retrograde today in your finances and values sector. Over the next few months, you will be required to learn some hard lessons about what's important to you. This will also involve your role in wider interest groups. Check your bank balance and start making more responsible decisions.

Monday 24th

The Moon drops into your social sector and brings intensity with it. You may have joined an interest group which deals with matters of life and concepts that are mysterious or hard to grasp. There is a dissonance coming from Uranus, who sits opposite the Moon; what's being shaken up?

Tuesday 25th

Today you may find that you're sifting through your friendships and assessing how much value they have for you. Saturn retrograde is connecting and asking you how far you are willing to go to get what you want. It's likely that you see some power struggles going on now.

Wednesday 26th

A Full Moon occurs in your hidden sector. What has come to light in this area now? Are you struggling to know where your path is? Have you seen a direction you wish to take? You may find that issues from the past return to be finished once and for all.

Thursday 27th

There is very tricky energy to manage today and you may feel isolated and frustrated. If it's possible, take some time out for meditation, yoga or physical exercise. Self-medicating may seem like an answer but will do you no favours. Stay connected and try to ground yourself.

. . . .

Friday 28th

The Moon dips into your sign and you feel like yourself again. It's important for you to be seen as hard-working and in control. Your shadow side wishes to be self-indulgent, but you must turn this around and focus on your social standing as a responsible person. Your self-talk may be negative today.

Saturday 29th

Mercury turns retrograde in your health and duties sector, today. He meets Venus and they discuss that the important thing for this period is that you take care of your own needs. There may be a tendency to burn out now. Make all the usual Mercury retrograde checks.

Sunday 30th

This morning you may be more relaxed and open to learning from others. This may be a distraction tactic to avoid doing necessary chores, but you will achieve something different. A little respite from being strict with yourself will do you good. Try to clear your head today.

Monday 31st

The Moon meets Saturn and you may meet someone who challenges you, today. There is an energetic exchange, and this may excite you and lead you to new ventures. Be mindful of personal boundaries and listen well. Be receptive and passive with people who are in authority or elders in your community.

JUNE
. . . .

Tuesday 1st

Today, the Sun meets the point of fate and you have an opportunity to reach into the future. What is calling you the loudest? What is making you excited? These feelings may be emphasised as the Moon meets expansive Jupiter. Start making plans to achieve your biggest dreams.

Wednesday 2nd

Venus enters your relationship sector, today. You will find that you are more likely to wish for harmony and keep the peace now. Some things are just not worth fighting over. The energy which Venus brings can be highly intuitive, so pay attention to dreams and symbols whilst she is here.

Thursday 3rd

When the Moon meets Neptune today you find that, far from getting a hold on your dreams, you may have to see them through the eyes of another. A different perspective will show you room for growth. Mercury connects, so beware of how you communicate today. Aim for clarity to avoid misunderstanding.

Friday 4th

Lovely energy from Venus and Jupiter can make this a very lucky day for you, regarding relationships and money. You may overspend on a luxury item or an enjoyable evening for two. Something may inspire you to be impulsive. This won't do you any harm. Light a spark today.

Saturday 5th

Today may be difficult as aggression and control issues surface. Mars sits opposite Pluto and you may see all-out war. You can use this energy in a different way and be creative or ruthless. Find something you no longer have a use for and transform it, or let it go completely.

Sunday 6th

Use your creative powers today. Jupiter and Venus are giving you their blessing, and this may mean that you find a way to make money or love. This energy is too good to lose, so make the effort to co-create something beautiful with a partner or alone.

Monday 7th

There is restlessness in the air which could be making you jumpy. This is not such a bad thing but Saturn, your ruler, is watching what you do with it. You have the potential to come up with something that is genius and innovative. Follow your gut and be unique today. You may surprise yourself.

Tuesday 8th

Today you're driven and controlled. You may have greater power and influence than usual but be sure not to abuse it. Jupiter connects, meaning that if you neglect or misuse this power, it will become larger than you intended, and then uncontrollable. Tread carefully and be responsible.

Wednesday 9th

The Moon in your health and duties sector connects to Saturn retrograde and asks that you put yourself last today. Saturn watches how you treat others and how far you're willing to go to be of service. If you can achieve this, it will be remembered at a later date.

Thursday 10th

Today there's a New Moon in your health and duties sector. This Moon also joins Mercury retrograde, so simply mull over any new goals and intentions. You may find that your good nature is being taken for granted and you must nip this in the bud before it escalates.

Friday 11th

Mercury is in the heart of the Sun and is saying nothing. This is your cue to do the same. You may be at the receiving end of other's troubles and must allow them to speak. It's also possible that you get a headache today from having a very busy mind.

Saturday 12th

The Moon in your relationship sector meets Venus. This weekend can be filled with loving kindness if you wish. The energy is there for you to lap up and let someone special nurture and comfort you. You may surprise yourself at how much you like letting go of control.

Sunday 13th

Mars has moved into your intimacy sector. You may find that your sex life moves up a new level. Mars will also take care of any shared finances or interests, and make sure that they are still working for you. The Moon here adds intensity to your self-expression.

Monday 14th

Today may be tough and there's a possibility that you get involved in arguments. You may have too much to say for yourself, or perhaps you're being rather brutish about getting your own way. This may all blow up in your face if you are not careful. Overspending is possible too.

. . . .

Tuesday 15th

Saturn and Uranus are squaring off. This energy will feel like a badly-behaved small child having a telling off and a subsequent tantrum. This may involve money or overstepping other people's personal boundaries. Play it safe and toe the line today; don't risk a catastrophic eruption.

Wednesday 16th

This morning may be calmer, but there is a chance that you are paying the price for yesterday. You may be dragged into the boss's office and asked to account for yourself. You're likely to recall every detail and can pinpoint the trigger that caused the outburst to happen.

Thursday 17th

Although there's a running theme of co-operation in the background, remember that Mercury is retrograde. You may feel some effects of this today as you inadvertently say the wrong thing to the wrong people. It may also be that you have solved a long-standing problem and you shout about it.

Friday 18th

The end of the week sees the Moon in your career sector. This is a lovely, harmonising Moon which can restore harmony after the agitation of the last few days. Whether you're in work or not, you regain self-control and continue to get active in your intimacy sector.

Saturday 19th

Today is best spent slowing down or kicking back and relaxing.
Try to spend the day by first doing what is necessary and then
allowing yourself some downtime. You may wish to be alone
and simply spoil yourself with food or movies that you love.
Get out the blanket tent for the day.

Sunday 20th

The Moon in your social sector beckons you out of hiding.
You may not enjoy being with others or interacting online,
because you were happy where you were. You may see control
issues or power struggles within your friendship groups.
Don't get involved, there will be trouble.

Monday 21st

The good news for today is that it's the Summer Solstice and the
Sun shifts into your relationship sector. This will be warming,
healing and nourishing. The bad news is that Jupiter turns
retrograde and will return to your finance sector. You may
already feel restrictions or blockages.

Tuesday 22nd

If you manage to loosen your grip today, you may enjoy a
glimpse of your inner compass once more. Watery, emotional
energy comes from the Moon, Venus and Neptune, and you are
open to merging with your wider friendship groups. You have
more empathy today and may be called upon to use it.

Wednesday 23rd

The Moon is now in your hidden sector but opposes Mercury, who is now direct. You may need to bite your tongue and refrain from expressing your views on helping or serving others. Control issues will surface from your relationship sector. Lie low and wait until this energy passes.

Thursday 24th

A Full Moon drops into your sign. You look at the last six months and wonder if you have achieved much personally. If you look back, you will see that yes, you are much further up that mountain of personal growth. Allow yourself a pat on the back and try not to underrate your accomplishments and achievements.

Friday 25th

Neptune turns retrograde today. This will have the effect of casting a fog over your true north. Don't worry too much about it; this is your chance to reassess and gather more information. There may be some pleasant surprises coming to you from your creative and romantic sector now.

Saturday 26th

In your sign, the Moon meets Pluto and you may feel a gut-wrenching instinct that something has ended. This is because the Moon is opposite Venus in your relationship sector. Your sense of balance and harmony may be momentarily rocked. This isn't as bad as you think, so stay calm.

Sunday 27th

Venus now enters your intimacy sector. The bump you felt
yesterday may have been your relationship leaving one way of
existing and moving to a new one. You will need adjustment
time, so go easy on yourself and your lover. Try not to take
anything personally today, as it's not meant that way.

Monday 28th

An outgoing Moon meets newly retrograde Jupiter. You may
need to use this period to go over financial matters or seek
legal advice. Jupiter can bring blessings, but also needs to
see fairness. Today there's a chance that you see what this
retrograde will involve.

Tuesday 29th

Your conversations may be like a hotline today. Your ability to
merge and connect with others may bring a large community
to a small space. This could be an online gathering or spiritual
meeting. Either way, there's potential to break down barriers
and bring people together in the name of love.

Wednesday 30th

The Moon meets Neptune today, who has cloaked himself
in secrecy. It may be frustrating, trying to access your inner
compass and return to your dreams. You must use this time to
look at other perspectives and ensure that you are on the path
that is meant for you.

JULY
. . . .

Thursday 1st

Today you are more inclined to make some noise. You may
need to get family members together and lay the law down.
Simple active encouragement will be enough to get things
moving today. There's a danger of being too pushy and
dominant, so take care that you are respectful.

Friday 2nd

You may have more success in organising a family gathering
today. This is because your powers of persuasion are back,
thanks to Mercury. Mars, your drive, is also making a more
favourable aspect. Your heart and mind are in sync and you
can lead others on an exciting expedition.

Saturday 3rd

After a good start, you may now feel that things have slowed
down or become stuck. You may not have looked at all the
details and are now blocked. Money may be an issue today
and could prevent you from moving forward. Be prepared to
possibly abandon your weekend plans.

Sunday 4th

You may have a mini tantrum today as nothing seems to be
going your way. In fact, you may feel like people have wasted
your valuable time. The Moon meets Uranus and, as you might
be feeling, this energy is highly unstable. You may experience
disapproval from an elder or boss.

Monday 5th

It's possible that you want to use up your restless, creative energy. Conditions enable you to dream and communicate with like-minded people. Encouragement will come from your relationship sector; see if you can co-create something unusual. This will take the edge off a disappointing weekend. You will be pleased about being productive.

Tuesday 6th

You may not be able to concentrate much today. Your mind is busy with duties and concepts you need to understand. This will clash with your dreams that are creeping in, as if to remind you of them. Clarity is far away, but this phase will soon pass. Be patient.

Wednesday 7th

The Moon makes nice connections to both Venus and Mars. Emotional stability and cooperation are possible between men and women. You may find that two seemingly opposite things are able to be merged easily. A barrier may come down and you are invited to explore. Tread carefully, now.

Thursday 8th

The Moon meets Mercury and your heart and head are balanced. There may still be a lot to think about and tick off your to-do list, but you manage this. Your dreams and visions continue to nag you, but you know that – without clarity – it is pointless to pursue them.

Friday 9th

The Moon is in your relationship sector and you may find that you snuggle down for the weekend and allow yourself to be cared for. Uranus connects from your creative and romantic sector. This means that time spent with a partner is fun and serves you both well.

Saturday 10th

Today there's a New Moon in your relationship sector. It opposes Pluto, which normally means you need to break free and be alone. However, if you stay comforted and protected, you may have the opportunity to set goals and intentions together. Share your dreams with a loved one.

Sunday 11th

The Moon slips into your intimacy sector, where you may get to know someone better. Don't be afraid to speak your mind now. Be bold but mindful of going too far. Mercury now enters your relationship sector. You will have much to discuss with a partner. Be caring and inquisitive.

Monday 12th

Mars and Venus are getting closer and the Moon passes both today. This is a very romantic day and you may walk side by side with a partner or important person. Your needs and those of another have equal importance and are being attended to. Don't risk rocking the boat today.

Tuesday 13th

The meeting of Mars and Venus occurs. You may experience a new level of relating, such as a matching of compassionate hearts and minds. No-one is more dominant today. You may find that this energy merges within you, and your emotional and rational sides meet in the middle.

Wednesday 14th

Think about how you may be of service to the wider world today. Is there something that you can do for others from a different country? You may like to learn a little about their culture, religion or philosophies. A taste of the exotic may be a nice treat for two this evening.

Thursday 15th

Today you may get some insight into how you could carry out your dreams and wishes. The Sun lets in just enough light over Neptune's fogs. You might discover realistic and useful ways of achieving your passions. You may wonder why you have never seen this before.

Friday 16th

It will be difficult to attain balance in the workplace today, because your relationships are causing barriers. You will need to talk things through and come to some sort of agreement or mediation. An elder may be trying to show you the best path, but you'll probably choose to ignore it.

Saturday 17th

The Moon connects to Mars and Venus, helping you to restore equilibrium. There are voices that need to be heard, including yours. Egos may clash and you may see power struggles, but you are at your best and can deal with it. Enjoy time out with friends this evening.

Sunday 18th

You may have intense feelings of jealousy around certain friendships now. Is there a group that seems to be preventing you from being yourself or speaking out? Uranus sits opposite the Moon and you may see a row develop. Watch your spending today; you could be overdoing it.

Monday 19th

Neptune is calling you to realign with your best self. This may be an emotional episode but will be brief and teach you something important. Take control of your feelings and let those ugly feelings go. This evening you need time alone to process your thoughts.

Tuesday 20th

Lovers or special friends can help you to navigate today. You may be feeling sorry for yourself and mourning chances you had but didn't take. Use this energy to make a vision board and see what really draws your attention. It may be something unusual or non-conforming. Broaden your horizons, if only in your mind.

Wednesday 21st

This is another lovely day for total agreement with a partner. You know what you want and know how to get it. The decision you need to make now is if you actually need it. Something is always stopping you from stepping out. Don't be too hard on yourself.

Thursday 22nd

As Venus enters your travel sector, she will help you to make solid plans or educate yourself on issues about the wider world. She asks if you may be of service to people in foreign lands somehow. The Sun moves into your intimacy sector and lights up dark corners.

Friday 23rd

The Moon in your sign may be making you more emotional than usual. Keep doing what you are doing, but honour these feelings. Your race to the top of your personal mountain does not have to be won in a single day. Pluto asks you to reconsider ambitions that no longer serve you.

Saturday 24th

A Full Moon in your finance and value sector highlights your sense of self-worth today. You may be thinking about joining a cause and doing something for the greater good. What have you built regarding finances in the last six months? You find that you discuss dreams with a loved one.

Sunday 25th

Difficult connections make you restless and irritable today. You may need to assess your opinions on something you have lately revealed to a partner, as they could now be causing a conflict. If you're feeling extra-anxious, stay away from others and spend some time alone.

Monday 26th

The Moon moves into your communications sector and you may find that connecting with like-minded people is important now. Your mood may be bigger than usual and out of proportion to the trigger that caused it. Loving yourself may seem a distant memory today. Try yoga or meditation and connect with spirit.

Tuesday 27th

There is lovely energy for you to access today. You may be drifting off to a fantasy land or simply relaxing more than you normally do. This may be good for you, as you can be too uptight and focused on your social standing sometimes. Make art, poetry or love today.

Wednesday 28th

Mercury has flown into your intimacy sector now. He will unearth some of your deepest treasures that you keep to yourself. Expect relating and communicating to become intense at this time. Jupiter has retrograded into your finance and value sector. Be very careful with spending while he's here.

Thursday 29th

Mars now joins Venus in your travel sector. He can give you the energy and drive to get things done. If you have a to-do list, you should fly through it now. He opposes Jupiter, so be sure to double-check every detail before going public with any new plans.

Friday 30th

Take it slowly today, as the energy is not favourable for rushing around. You may face a challenge to your person and need to change an outlook or attitude. Earthy energy gives you a rest and lets you ground yourself. You may be much more realistic and practical today.

Saturday 31st

Nothing much will be achieved today, so take the day off. Your creative juices aren't flowing and everything that comes out of your mouth sounds wrong. You may upset someone in authority or a leader in your wider interest groups. Be silent until this energy passes, as it will soon.

AUGUST

. . . .

Sunday 1st

Stay in a safe place and get inspired. Mercury is silent but sends subtle messages that can be fuel for your creative juices. When the Moon sits with Uranus, you may receive a breakthrough and become unstuck. There will be no stopping you then. Follow your dreams and create, or alternatively use this time to get romantic.

Monday 2nd

You have a rebellious streak in you. Your words may be bordering on the taboo or bad taste, but you feel they serve your purpose. Ego clashes are likely, but you can rise above them. Duties and obligations fill your day and you may begrudge the mundane things you do.

Tuesday 3rd

If you're clever, today may be beneficial to you in the long run. Seek out people who can take you away from your day-to-day life and show you the deeper mysteries of the world. An attachment to something ethereal may do you some good. Use today to explore things that are different, and explore them differently.

Wednesday 4th

Be very careful today, as there's a chance that you speak out of turn and cause an upset. Mercury is rooting around in your intimacy sector and may reveal a secret or two. You have little interest in surrendering and going with the flow. Today you go your own way, despite the possible consequences.

Thursday 5th

Take some downtime and relax with a partner or close friend. The planets favour emotional and sexual activity for you. Today you simply want your needs met and this may be as simple as cooking a favourite meal and sharing it with someone special. Nurture yourself and a significant other.

Friday 6th

You may feel powerless if you allow yourself to relax into another's control. This is your sticking point. If you can get over this and receive a kindness in the way it is meant, you will release stress and tension. Share your dreams and visions with your lover.

Saturday 7th

The Moon drops into your intimacy sector, letting you take back self-control. This is a time where the giving and taking in relationships are easier. However, the Sun in this sector clashes with Uranus. This can mean sexual fireworks or a big misunderstanding. Work a problem through before nightfall.

Sunday 8th

A New Moon shows up and gives you the chance to make a fresh start with someone close. It's a good time to put all your cards on the table and have your say. Saturn sits opposite, making this an uncomfortable experience, but it will be worth it in the long run.

Monday 9th

This morning you may find that you have a lot to say. This will be truly heartfelt, and it's better that you speak rather than hold it in. With Jupiter sitting opposite, you could be prone to over-exaggeration, so try to stick to the facts and be brutally honest.

Tuesday 10th

You are emotionally driven to get things right, today. It may feel as if you're fighting for a cause all by yourself, but this is untrue. You're looking after number one and others will need to see this. Communications may not be the best today; misunderstandings are possible.

Wednesday 11th

The Moon meets Venus and you're extra emotional, and maybe a little selfish too. You may feel that there's much more to life due to you and question the fairness in this. You may decide to do something about this now. Take back control of what you desire.

Thursday 12th

Balance and harmony come back to you, if only in small doses. You're composed enough to get through your workday. Mercury has entered your travel sector, where he will aid you in seeking out higher truths and exploring new lands and cultures. Be of service to yourself while he is here.

Friday 13th

Today your heart is peaceful, and you relax more. You may be looking at how your work and career restricts your movements and personal growth. This is out of character for a high-flyer like you, so you may wish to keep it to yourself for now.

Saturday 14th

Enjoy some weekend time with friends and explore new possibilities. You may have one or two very close and intense friendships who never fail you when your topics of conversation are unconventional. Talk your feelings through and try to gain some clarity on your current restlessness. This will be a good outlet.

Sunday 15th

Uranus is sending you mixed emotions and nervous energy that you must act on. Be mindful that any emotions you are already feeling will be exaggerated by a connection to Jupiter. Watch your spending today too, as this may be where the Uranus blow-out happens.

Monday 16th

As the week begins, you may wish to set aside some time to process your recent feelings. The Moon supports this by dropping into your hidden sector where solitary time is better spent. Your emotions may roller-coaster today, but this will pass as quickly as the Moon. Stick with it and breathe deeply.

Tuesday 17th

Today you may find that it is difficult to align yourself with your true north, however hard you try. Stop trying; this is a time of surrender and not control. Everything will happen naturally, so forcing issues today is futile as it will not get you anywhere.

Wednesday 18th

The Moon squares off with Venus, who is now in your career sector. You may be evaluating your persona in the workplace and seeing it as a mask that does not really represent who you are. Don't put yourself down; you work hard to get to the top and this is highly commended.

Thursday 19th

The Moon in your sign is rattling some nerves, making you anxious and restless. Mercury meets Mars, which can mean that you're talking your talk or being passive-aggressive. With Uranus turning retrograde today, it is likely to be the latter. Put your money where your mouth is or stay silent.

Friday 20th

The Sun is in the final part of your intimacy sector. Make sure that issues here are completed, especially money matters you may share with another. You have the urge to see exactly where you have control, and will deal with areas that need more attention today.

Saturday 21st

The Moon is squaring off with newly retrograde Uranus. Your ideas of what is valuable to you may be up for review today. You may spend the weekend having a clear-out and minimising your possessions. This will make space and feel fresh. It could be an uplifting activity to do.

Sunday 22nd

A Full Moon lights up your sector regarding finances and value. If you have decided to declutter your personal space, you will now see that this is a result of something you started six months ago. You may have to be ruthless and let things go, but the time is right.

Monday 23rd

The Moon in your communication sector may see you connecting with people you may have been neglecting lately. Although this may sound lovely, be warned that it could take a nasty turn. There may be a trigger that is activated, and a long-standing grudge reappears.

Tuesday 24th

As much as you wish to spread the love and be there for all, you can't. You may feel divided and conflicted today. The Moon meets Neptune, who confuses you. It's likely that you question loyalties and may need to make some sacrifices. Be mindful of your words today, as they may unintentionally hurt.

Wednesday 25th

You may be stimulated to act now. A head full of plans is great if you can manifest them. Double-check and look at what is entirely unrealistic. You may get drawn into family matters that conflict with your own personal agenda. Stand back and be silent if you must.

Thursday 26th

Family members may drain you today as they need you to take control of an issue. This will be difficult for you to do and you may have to say no. Declining invitations may be necessary to simply preserve your own energy. Keep a low profile if need be.

Friday 27th

This morning you may awake with your creative juices flowing. You need something grounding and practical to do today. Getting your hands dirty with art, gardening or DIY can be satisfying. You may ignore your duties and do your own thing while it is filling your mind now.

Saturday 28th

You have a lot of restless energy to use up, so consider art, decorating or decluttering for the weekend. This may help to balance your nerves, which may be highly strung at the moment. Peaceful activities such as colouring or walking will also help to bring you back into alignment.

Sunday 29th

If you're choosing to do practical things this weekend, you will notice that you feel in total control of yourself and your emotions. Note this and store it away for another time when you feel restless or out of balance. There's nothing you like more than being in control.

Monday 30th

You are more than happy to begin the working week and maintain your regular schedule. This actually gives you a sense of normality. Although you may have many options, you manage to choose and stick to a routine that benefits you. Mercury enters your career sector and helps with this.

Tuesday 31st

Today you're in two minds. You're getting nudges from Neptune, who wants you to recall your dreams and visions. Likewise, Mars is calling you to act responsibly and do your duties. You receive help today from someone who may be an elder or associated with the law.

SEPTEMBER

. . . .

Wednesday 1st

A midweek break or date with a partner may be on your mind, but work responsibilities are likely to make it difficult. There may be many chores to finish before you can settle down and receive soul nourishment from someone close. Get things done and enjoy an evening of relaxation.

Thursday 2nd

The energy today can be excitable, but once again your work duties could prevent you from fully enjoying it until this evening. Mars sits opposite Neptune, making you undecided whether to share and merge when communicating, or keep things to yourself. This may result in passive-aggressive behaviour. Conversations may be strained as you do not get clarity from others.

Friday 3rd

This is the time of the month where you want to break free from the confines of another and assert your own authority. Keeping a low profile will help to avoid any unnecessary conflict. Allowing yourself to be drawn back to your true north will bring you back to yourself.

Saturday 4th

A deeply intimate Moon has you questioning your rights and striving to put your point forward. You have the gift of the gab but must be mindful not to cross personal boundaries when dealing with those in authority, as this may result in tempers being raised. You might find this challenging.

Sunday 5th

You receive help from Venus, who restores your sense of balance and harmony. You may have finished a work project that has eaten into your weekend. However, now that you have got it out of the way, you are free to enjoy your evening. Talk to your interest groups today.

Monday 6th

There may be some changes that are difficult to implement today. Venus and Pluto are squaring off, and this means that you may be presented with a control issue at work that threatens to undermine you. Don't be scapegoated against your wishes.

Tuesday 7th

An important New Moon occurs today in your travel sector. This is also where you are of service to others or taken for granted. You may feel anger rising when the Moon meets Mars, so it is important that you keep your head and don't let yourself down by acting out.

Wednesday 8th

This morning feels like a new start. You may have said goodbye to something that was no longer in your best interest. Putting your best foot forward and climbing that mountain may seem an arduous task, but it is a start to better and brighter things for you.

Thursday 9th

You have a head full of conversation. This may be your own self-talk and you must be careful not to put yourself down right now. You are worthy and you are recognised for the influence you have in the workplace. Believe it or not, you are the harmonising influence that others look up to.

Friday 10th

Venus spends her last few hours in your career sector. Her energy
will help you to recognise your own worth. She will leave this
sector knowing that you are at peace with yourself and recognise
that you do a good job. She enters your social sector ready to
seduce and party.

Saturday 11th

That restless energy returns, but you should now know what
to do with it. As it's the weekend and the Moon is in your
social sector, dancing or enjoying a meal with friends could
be the answer. Connect with those who appreciate your dark
sense of humour.

Sunday 12th

Conversations with friends and interest groups can be heated
but exciting. Be careful though, as things may get out of hand
if not monitored properly. When the Moon drops into your
hidden sector, you will want to have some time to yourself and
organise your thoughts.

Monday 13th

As you can't get clarity on your dreams, visions or true north
today, stick to using your mind for work projects. Working
from home may give you the peace you need to get things
straight. Use your time wisely and don't be tempted to
daydream the hours away.

Tuesday 14th

The Sun is opposite Neptune today and you may get more clarity on a communication problem or see a glimpse of your dreams again. There's a chance of aggression or conflict which can get out of hand. This afternoon, you're more in control and enjoy learning from friends.

Wednesday 15th

The Moon in your sign is a great chance to present yourself to important people or have meetings which can be beneficial to you. Mars has marched into your career sector, making you a force to be reckoned with. Just don't take advantage and become power-hungry, or everything you have worked towards will backfire on you.

Thursday 16th

Today is an excellent day for taking back control or simply being your own boss. You know what you want to achieve today and have the energy to do so. You may lead a group in a project for the greater good, as you are the right person for the job.

Friday 17th

You may have to be cruel to be kind today. The energy is tricky and may feel restricting. This can make you anxious, as it means upsetting someone you hold in great esteem. Your social sector and creative sector will feel the brunt of this today.

Saturday 18th

Take a rest today and recharge your batteries. You may be feeling overemotional due to recent events, but also because Jupiter is with the Moon. Connect with spirit and serve yourself some soul food. Speaking to your interest groups may help you to come back in alignment with yourself.

Sunday 19th

Conversations may feel surreal today, but this is fine as you don't need a heavy day. You may find yourself at a crossroads, but only a minor one. Look at how far you have come this year and how you would like to move on. Venus is seducing you with social activities today.

Monday 20th

A late Full Moon in your communications sector may throw the spotlight on recent events. Evaluating this may show you that there have been subtle movements towards a more connected way of interacting for most of the year. Try to look at everything from a different perspective today.

Tuesday 21st

Today you're more active and positive. You may need to see to family matters which will conflict with your own interests, but you do this happily. Your sense of leadership in the family helps you to move everyone along in the right direction. This may be a valuable lesson for some.

Wednesday 22nd

Today is the Autumn Equinox, and day and night are equal lengths. Use this time to pause and reflect before jumping into the winter months and shorter days. Plan for activities that can be achieved in a shorter time scale now. Be mindful of how you communicate today.

Thursday 23rd

This may be a difficult day to navigate. Your social groups may have some issues and there may be arguments. You would be advised to stay away from the drama if you are not directly involved. Bitching and gossiping may be the nature of the conflict. Don't join in.

Friday 24th

The Moon is in your creative sector and has met Uranus. You should know by now that this means you are feeling some sort of restlessness and must do something with this fidgety energy. Be sure to use this energy wisely as your ruler Saturn is watching and will not be kind to you if you abuse it.

Saturday 25th

Mercury turns retrograde tomorrow in your career sector. Use today to make all the necessary preparations. Back up all your devices and double-check travel plans. You will be revising a lot of work projects over the next three weeks. You can handle this; not everyone can.

Sunday 26th

Mercury retrograde begins. This does not bother you as you are busy making plans for the future. You are mindful not to act on anything yet, and to keep all plans on the back-burner for now. You're energised and happy to do your duties today. Connect with those you have neglected.

Monday 27th

Today would be a good day to check in with your health. The Moon sits in your health and duties sector and is quite peaceful. You may often forget about looking after your body and work yourself too hard. Take the time to make sure you're all in working order.

Tuesday 28th

The Moon connects to Mercury retrograde, so watch out that the trickster planet doesn't trip you up. Stay alert for miscommunications and make sure that everyone is on the same page. Think before you respond and only do so if it's true, kind and helpful. Say nothing if you are unsure.

Wednesday 29th

A midweek date with someone you love or admire will be good for you today. You may be feeling a little tense and wish to relinquish control. A parent figure or someone who knows how to look after your needs will be of great help today.

Thursday 30th

There's a huge amount of watery, emotional energy today. This may unsettle you. The best thing you can do is to allow yourself to go with the flow. Resistance is futile and you may even find that you enjoy the energy if you can embrace it. Surrender and merge with this beautiful energy.

OCTOBER

. . . .

Friday 1st

Get ready for a weekend of close connections and deeper intimacy.
You must always remember to be respectful of other's boundaries.
Today, you have the right amount of curiosity, energy and courage
to take steps that you have deemed too big for you in the past.
Be adventurous and explore life's mysteries.

Saturday 2nd

Be good and take smaller steps if you notice that you're triggering
someone. It can be challenging today as you may be invited into a
confidence, but then not know where the borders are. Seductive
Venus may help you loosen up a little today.

Sunday 3rd

Mercury retrograde connects to Jupiter, making any mishaps
much larger and possibly off the scale. Tread carefully around
work issues and always aim for balance and understanding.
Read between the lines in conversations. This is also a good
day to detox, declutter or do something else that is good for
your body.

Monday 4th

You may be torn between short-term and long-term goals
today. What satisfies you, for now, isn't what's usual for you,
and you know this. Inspiration from your travel and higher
education sector may provide you with a new artistic or
romantic pursuit. Others will be pleasantly surprised.

Tuesday 5th

Today you may have to be strict about how much you give to others. Your time may be in demand, but you must look after number one. You may consider letting go of things which are no longer good for you, including bad habits, coping mechanisms and outdated thinking.

Wednesday 6th

A New Moon in your career sector allows you to set goals and intentions around your work and aspirations. This Moon also contacts Mars and Mercury; this is a great day to ask for a rise or to get a review. Pluto turns direct too. Feel the pressure lift from your sector of self.

Thursday 7th

Venus enters your hidden sector now, where she will entice you to do more introspection and self-care. You may feel this intensely and might react with anticipation and defensiveness. Feel your way into it but ensure that you allow yourself plenty of alone time now, even if just to spoil yourself.

Friday 8th

The Sun and Mars meet and make a powerhouse of great energy in your career sector. Projects will likely steam ahead and be successful now. Be careful today, as someone in your social circle may upset you. There may be a nasty edge to this person.

Saturday 9th

Today is all about communications. Mercury is in the heart of the Sun and receiving new information. Your job is to listen and not speak. He's sitting with Mars, so you may feel restless and find it almost impossible not to say anything. Keep your mouth zipped.

Sunday 10th

Saturn, your ruler, goes direct today. This is good news, as you will now feel more forward motion regarding finances and value. Spend some time alone and readjust your thoughts. A weight has been lifted and you have been given the green light. Try to pick up on clues and messages from Mercury.

Monday 11th

Your private time will benefit from a little detective work today. There could be something that has been hidden from you, but is now coming to the surface. A search for truth and justice may begin to yield results. You may be wishing to break free from old habitual patterns.

Tuesday 12th

This is a quiet day where you might decide to pick up your artistic endeavours and get creative. Cooking exotic dishes or adding sensuous furnishings to your home can help you feel grounded. The Moon is in your sign and you may like to treat yourself now. And why not?

Wednesday 13th

Newly-direct Pluto greets the Moon and you notice what has left your life in the past few months. This may not be something you wished for but Pluto, who deals with permanent endings, has done it for you. Is there space for something new and exciting to come in?

Thursday 14th

Saturn is your teacher today and you may find that
you're reviewing issues around money, social groups and
rebelliousness. Have you learned anything from Saturn's
retrograde? You are often too strict on yourself; now is the
time to loosen the reins a little. Splash out on something nice.

Friday 15th

You may see some issues with bosses or persons in authority
today. Jupiter hosts the Moon and expands any mood you're
currently feeling. It is likely that you over-inflate your own
ego and get uptight. Take a deep breath and be humble, as you
possibly need to apologise now.

Saturday 16th

Today you are more forgiving and can go with the flow more
easily. You may be talking to those who inspire you to dream or
get spiritual. Short visits can be a labour of love or a personal
quest to an end goal. Pause and reflect before making any
definitive choices.

Sunday 17th

Jupiter turns direct today. That is another heavyweight
shifted from your finances and value sector. A lawsuit may
have come to completion or an annoying big-head might
be exposed. Take some time to realign yourself as the Moon
meets Neptune. You may see something worth pursuing,
even though Neptune is still retrograde.

Monday 18th

Mercury joins the others and turns direct, giving you some breathing space in the workplace. You may need to go over the events of the last three weeks and look at where Mercury has called for a review, a redo, or a recall. Now you have the chance to put it all right.

Tuesday 19th

You may be action-orientated today, and eager to get on and do the things that the retrogrades have somehow prevented you doing. Take small steps and don't rush to do everything all at once. It's possible that you're bombarded with instructions or messages to deal with today.

Wednesday 20th

Today there's a Full Moon in your family sector. How many of your plans from the last six months have come to fruition? Celebrate those that have and don't mourn the ones that haven't. You may feel momentarily tired, exhausted even, but if you rest you will soon be back on your feet.

Thursday 21st

Restless energy fills you up and you have the urge to dance, rebel or do something artistic. Some of the ideas you have today will be too radical or unconventional so look to what is sensible. Use this energy to produce something beautiful or to speak words of love.

Friday 22nd

Mars and Pluto are squaring off today and you may see power struggles or control issues surfacing. This may be at work, as your status may be challenged. However, if you can look at things differently, there may be a workaround and a happy outcome for everyone involved.

Saturday 23rd

The Sun enters your social sector now. It's possible that your interest groups widen and the topics you choose to share become more obscure or taboo. You may look at the darker side of life and get involved with people who have esoteric knowledge. This may be a very secretive time.

Sunday 24th

Today is one of those days where you run around doing a lot of things for other people and have no time for yourself. You may have a list of chores to get through and can only rest at bedtime. Ensure that you don't get exhausted by making sure that you take short breaks throughout the day.

Monday 25th

Your dreams and visions seem too far away today. You're likely to question whether they are all just a mirage. Plan to share time with a lover or special person this evening. Your need to be nurtured, if only for a short while, may surface tonight. Let yourself be looked after.

Tuesday 26th

If you can possibly let yourself relax and be cared for today, you may receive a pleasant surprise. Your head and heart are not in agreement, so don't even try reconciling them. Have a dreamy day with someone who cares for you. Messages of support and encouragement will satisfy you.

Wednesday 27th

You may have had enough of being nurtured now and hit the limit of your patience. You might struggle to break free, but you must remember to be kind and give gratitude to others. Venus is asking that you come back to yourself and process things alone.

Thursday 28th

It's likely that you lack the energy today and sink deeper into dependency on someone special. You will find this difficult and feel like you have let yourself down. Turn towards spiritual practices when you need to feel connected, as you might find people to be too much for you at these times.

Friday 29th

Today you may be too bold for your own good. You're outspoken and aggressive. You're possibly boastful or obnoxious today. Mercury connects to the Moon, giving you the power of speech, but it may not go down the way you wish it to. Back off or erupt, it's your choice.

Saturday 30th

Mars enters your social sector. Expect there to be some heated discussions while he's here. Things are already intense in your friendship groups and you may see some splits or witness friendships dissolve. This evening you want to analyse what happened. Was there something you missed?

Sunday 31st

The Moon and Sun make a helpful connection for you to do some detective work. You may be scrutinising recent events and looking at every detail. It's possible that you unearth something that may be seen as radical, but in a good way. You seek truth and justice, and you may just get that.

NOVEMBER
. . . .

Monday 1st
Mercury and Jupiter combine to make your words count today.
It's possible that you're standing up for the underdog at work
or stating your own case. Either way, this will go well for you.
Money matters may be raised, so be sure to check out your
bank balance and work budgets

Tuesday 2nd
A harmonising Moon in your careers sector makes a helpful
connection to Saturn, the teacher planet. As he's your ruler,
there will be something you must pay attention to and take
on board. Bosses, elders or other leaders will be involved.
Control what you say, or there may be trouble.

Wednesday 3rd
The Moon meets Mercury today. There's something on your
mind which you feel so passionate about that you need to get
it off your chest. It's not advisable to do so right now; this may
churn in your mind until you have the right time to speak up.

Thursday 4th
After meeting Mars, the aggressive planet, the Moon becomes
new in your social sector. This can be a tricky time, where you
realise the need to make changes or end certain friendships
which have become volatile or stale. Venus urges you to put
yourself first and release some stress.

Friday 5th

Venus enters your sign. She will ensure that you are hard-working but remain kind to yourself. Mercury now enters your social sector. There will be a tendency to gossip now, and some malicious rumours may be spread. Stay away if you aren't directly involved as things could get nasty.

Saturday 6th

You may be attempting to mediate between friends or other social groups. Alternatively, you may be fighting for your place in the group. You may have a lot of processing to do before you fully understand this situation. Now isn't the time to act. Be responsible and respectful, always.

Sunday 7th

It will be difficult to see another point of view today. Thoughts may be keeping you awake at night and you just can't still your mind. You may be feeling self-righteous or indignant. The truth will come out if you're patient, as the culprit will be exposed soon.

Monday 8th

The Moon meets Venus in your sign. Indulge yourself with this soft feminine energy and look at ways to self-soothe. Your reputation is important to you and you are defending it strongly. Today, you may see a difference or a shift in the way you're perceived.

Tuesday 9th

Maybe it's time to let someone or something go now. You've worked hard for long enough, but have you seen the results you desire? Neptune draws you back to your inner compass. If something doesn't feel right, then it isn't in alignment and you must transform or discard it.

Wednesday 10th

This is an unfavourable day for friendship groups. There may be a feeling of the group joining for a common purpose, but look deeper. People may have their own agendas, and all are at odds. Harsh words may be spoken when Mars and Mercury meet. Elders will frown upon the young.

Thursday 11th

If a legal situation has come to a head, there may be unexpected results. If you want to raise a revolution, then this is the day to do it. Otherwise, get out of the crowd that is antagonising the system and keep your reputation clean. Don't get involved.

Friday 12th

Your true north is in sight today, so grab it with both hands. This may be your saving grace. Take a different approach to achieve your goals. You may have realised recently that you have been climbing the wrong mountain. Take some time out for a solitary practice such as meditation.

Saturday 13th

Mercury opposes Uranus, so there's still the possibility of upset or spiteful words between friends. However, this can be softened when the Moon meets Neptune, as you have the chance to see another side to things. You may also be strict and dispose of what is not serving you now.

Sunday 14th

What you want and what you feel are in sync today, and this helps you to put plans into action. Family may be supportive or need encouragement from you to get things going. It's up to you to make the change you need in your life right now.

Monday 15th

You may have a little setback today and discover that there is more work to be done than you first thought. Your social groups are coming back into order. Take your responsibilities seriously and make plans to give yourself more downtime.

Tuesday 16th

An intense day may leave you with a headache. You are on top form and doing what it takes to make a permanent change. However, this may leave you feeling drained and exhausted by the end of the day, so be sure to factor in some time to rest or switch off before bedtime.

Wednesday 17th

Today you may seek solace in your artistic pursuits. Mars sits opposite Uranus and this restless, volatile energy needs to create something. If you have no projects in mind, a good home-cooked meal with special friends will suffice. You may also wish to move your body with some exercise.

Thursday 18th

The Moon meets Uranus and you may now feel conflicted. Where did your energy go? Mercury fills your head with nonsense and Neptune draws you to dream impossible dreams. This will soon pass, so simply go with the flow and see where it takes you today. Stay safe and close to the shore.

Friday 19th

The build-up to the Full Moon today has been intense and may have knocked you from your centre. The best thing you can do would be to ground yourself with practical earthy activities. Look at what you have created in the last six months and celebrate your successes and achievements.

Saturday 20th

You may feel that you need a quiet weekend. Stick to your mundane duties and obligations and gently work through your list of chores. There may be a choice of things at the end of the day to help you relax. Some casual chat with friends or siblings will while away the hours.

Sunday 21st

You are commended on your sense of duty today. Take pride in the way you ensure that the people important to you have all they need and are OK. Calling on elders in the family will be gratifying for both you and them. Think rationally and logically now.

Monday 22nd

The Moon has shifted into your relationship sector and you may choose to spend time with a partner or close friend. Venus and Mars support any romantic connections you have today. The Sun has entered your hidden sector. What dark corners will it shine on to be healed?

Tuesday 23rd

You'll need to let someone take the lead today. This may unsettle you as you're a natural leader, but will ultimately let you have some breathing space. The energy is emotional and fluid, so spend time feeling, relating and connecting on a level that is not that familiar to you.

Wednesday 24th

Mercury joins the Sun in your hidden sector. Listen to your dreams now, as there may be important messages and clues there for you. You break away from connecting with a loved one and may have learned how to do this without causing an upset. It's time for your voice to be heard.

Thursday 25th

Mars and Venus are connecting well to make relating easy. The Moon is in your intimacy sector and you can speak your truth without fear. This is a good day for romance if you're respectful and mindful of personal boundaries.

Friday 26th

You may look at what's important to you now. It's possible that this has changed over the course of the year. Group ventures may not be as good as you first thought. Insist on speaking your mind, but do so with compassion. Truth and justice have come to mean more to you than they once did.

Saturday 27th

It may be time for a declutter or detox. If you are studying, you may wish to go through your notes at this time, as you will see more details and omissions now. Your mind and heart are not in sync, so time is better spent alone. Take some time out to get your cluttered mind into a place where you feel it needs to be.

Sunday 28th

Stay in the mindset of being methodical and you may see that your workload decreases. This is you being more efficient and giving your attention to practical, honest work. External dramas can be too distracting for you. Get the job done today with no daydreaming.

Monday 29th

Once again, Mercury is in the heart of the Sun. If you're observant, you may notice subtle messages or hints enter your awareness. This is Mercury's way of telling you what he has found in your psyche and what needs to come up for healing. Note this for a later date.

Tuesday 30th

Your ruler, Saturn, is connecting to the Sun and Mercury. This means that your next lesson may be hard work, but ultimately essential to your self-development. You have a little time to dream today; Venus and Neptune let you realign with your inner compass and you feel satisfied with your progress.

DECEMBER

. . . .

Wednesday 1st

Finishing up work projects is possible this morning, with the Moon in your career sector. Tie up loose ends and make sure that everyone is on the same page. This afternoon, Neptune finally turns direct and you will now be able to make some great forward shifts to get closer to your true north.

Thursday 2nd

This is a great day to come to terms with anything that is intense or difficult for you to process. When you do your best, you will be perceived well by others. This may be challenging if you resist authority and can cause conflict, so play by the rules.

Friday 3rd

The Moon meets Mars in your social sector. This can have the effect of getting your friends together for a vigorous activity, but may also mean that aggression or tempers are likely. You may come up against a big character who likes to throw their weight around. Keep your own temper under control.

Saturday 4th

There is a New Moon in your hidden sector today. Spending time alone and making a personal agenda for the coming year will help you form new plans. You may like to spread your wings a bit more. Listen to what Mercury has to say when he meets the Moon. Think logically and rationally today.

Sunday 5th

The Moon makes a great connection to Jupiter, who tells you to think big. Whatever you secretly desire for your self-improvement will be enhanced. There is also the possibility of enjoying your alone time so much that you stay in solitude a little longer than normal. This won't do you any harm.

Monday 6th

Mars in your social sector connects to Pluto. These two together can bring sudden change or events that are spontaneous and unexpected. It's possible that a friendship will end, or you disconnect from a group that has proved disappointing. Tune in to your own needs and wants and get back on course.

Tuesday 7th

The Moon meets Pluto in your sign, and you may get confirmation that something has outlived its usefulness to you. You may grieve the loss of this, but remain hopeful that you have done the right thing. You must stick to your guns and not back down.

Wednesday 8th

Today may be difficult, as the planetary energy is restless and restrictive. Trouble is stirred up easily. Someone in your social circle can make a scene today which could involve more people than is needed. You may have a brush with the law or need professional help in some way.

Thursday 9th

Look at your finances today. The upset in your social sector
may have drained your resources. Your wider interest groups
may also be affected. Give yourself plenty of time to get
your thoughts together before approaching someone with a
reprimand. This afternoon, you should feel more connected to
the collective.

Friday 10th

Give yourself a break today and dispose of some of your restless
energy. Speak your mind by all means, but find a way of doing
so that is respectful. You may wish to write things down and
present an idea, a concept or a letter of complaint.

Saturday 11th

Venus meets Pluto today. This can be seen as manipulation,
passive-aggression or power struggles. Watch out for this and
stay alert. The Moon meets newly-direct Neptune. If you get
sight of your dreams, hold onto them and start making plans
to manifest them. Your self-talk can be overwhelming today.

Sunday 12th

The Moon is now in your family sector. You may need to get active
and take a role in the upcoming festivities. Get your planner out
and schedule the weeks ahead with your tribe. Venus is still with
Pluto, so be mindful that you could potentially get coaxed into
doing something.

Monday 13th

Mars marches into your hidden sector and will not stay still. You may have some restless nights while he's here. Likewise, Mercury enters your sign. Your powers of communication will be on top form now. You're likely to experience a few weeks of racing thoughts with these two shifts.

Tuesday 14th

Get creative or productive today. You may have a need to treat yourself or buy in some good foods for the holiday season. There's a chance that you overspend, so be careful. If you do, you will probably need to justify this to yourself at a later date; be sensible.

Wednesday 15th

Have you bent the rules today? The Moon sits with Uranus and you're feeling rebellious. A person in authority is watching and isn't impressed. Perhaps your own self-indulgence has got the better of you. Is that luxury purchase really necessary? Think twice before being impulsive.

Thursday 16th

You'll possibly find yourself feeling more positive today. The control issues may have turned around to your advantage. It's likely that you have made the first step towards claiming your true north and feel good about this. Don't worry if you have upset someone in the process, they'll get over it.

Friday 17th

As the weekend approaches, you'll probably feel that your list of chores is endless. There may be a lot to prepare for the festive season and you find yourself running around. This could trigger you to want to be alone and do your own thing, but this isn't possible right now. Is there something you can do for yourself without neglecting your other duties?

Saturday 18th

If you feel as if you have already lost sight of your dreams, remember that the bigger life is pretty busy at this time and you simply need to go with the flow. There will be time for your dream plans later. Work through your to-do list today.

Sunday 19th

Venus turns retrograde in your sign. You may have issues around love or maintaining harmony now. It's possible that an old lover makes a reappearance. A Full Moon in your health and duties sector could highlight a troublesome health problem, or else show you where you do too much for others.

Monday 20th

You turn to a close friend or lover for some peace today. Your heart and head are at odds, and you may say something out of the blue. Soothing company and good food will take your mind off things. Allow yourself to be nurtured until you feel ready to face the world again.

Tuesday 21st

The Winter Solstice arrives. Today is best spent being cosy and warm with a loved one. The Sun enters your sign as if to agree with this. This longest night may have you contemplating the year gone by and sharing thoughts and dreams with a lover or close friend.

Wednesday 22nd

The courageous Moon in your intimacy sector is getting you ready for the celebrations. You may be stepping out and partying already. You want to say what is on your mind, regardless of the consequences. Be mindful that you don't upset someone you care a lot for. Don't be too impulsive.

Thursday 23rd

Jupiter is at the end of your finance and value sector. This is a critical time and you might just blow the bank. Be very careful with your spending, as Jupiter can exaggerate everything. This goes for your waistline, too. Your indulgent side may go overboard today.

Friday 24th

You have a need to check that everything is ready for the big celebrations. This can be a day filled with tension and arguments, as you might expect. The planets are not being very helpful. Everyone has their own agenda, so try to come to some sort of agreement with your nearest and dearest.

Saturday 25th

However you celebrate, be respectful and kind to those sharing your day. There is a tendency to take over or dominate, as Venus has met Pluto again. Put your own dreams aside and do your bit. Uranus and Mercury connect and herald a day of surprises and pleasant communication.

Sunday 26th

You may have reconnected with a person who is sympathetic to your vision for self-improvement. It's likely that you are discussing this in great detail today. You're in total control of what you want and know how you're going to go about getting it. Good for you.

Monday 27th

Today may be a little more peaceful and allow you time to be quiet and listen to your thoughts. Someone may have recently given you food for thought. Your mood may be a nice balance of satisfaction and anticipation. Give respect where it's due and listen to your elders.

Tuesday 28th

Make sure that you're not coming across as a control freak. Your mouth might run away with you today and you could become a bossy boots. No-one will thank you for this right now. Watch your ego, as it's likely to become over-inflated today. This will not do you any favours.

Wednesday 29th

Jupiter finally returns to your communication sector. He will stay here for the next twelve months, so think big, plan big, and stretch your boundaries now. Your energy is sociable but pushy today. You may breach a personal boundary and upset someone close. There is a sting in your words.

Thursday 30th

Mercury meets Pluto today. If you can't say something nice, you're better off saying nothing. Mercury will accept his new mission for you now, so look out for signs. The secretive, intense Moon in your social sector is emotionally attached to this. This will be about self-respect, self-control and owning your power.

Friday 31st

The end of the year is here, and you find that you look back and evaluate the year gone by. The Moon sits with Mars in your hidden sector. You may be wound up or anxious. Get out and join in the fun. Be a party animal tonight.

Capricorn

....

PEOPLE WHO SHARE
YOUR SIGN

PEOPLE WHO
SHARE YOUR SIGN
....

Dignified, self-sufficient, and determined, the perseverance and patience of Capricorns makes them often take first place in whatever they set their mind to. Take the King of Rock, Elvis Presley and world-renowned physicist Stephen Hawking as just two examples of what the persevering Capricorn can achieve. Discover which of these established Capricorns share your exact birthday and see if you can spot the similarities.

22nd December
Meghan Trainor (1993), Shiori Kutsuna (1992), Jordin Sparks (1989), Chris Carmack (1980), Vanessa Paradis (1972), Dina Meyer (1968), Ralph Fiennes (1962), Jean-Michel Basquiat (1960), Héctor Elizondo (1936)

23rd December
Harry Judd (1985), Jodie Marsh (1978), Corey Haim (1971), Carla Bruni (1967), Eddie Vedder (1964), Dave Murray (1956), Carol Ann Duffy (1955), Emperor Akihito of Japan (1933), Madam C. J. Walker (1867), Joseph Smith (1805)

24th December
Louis Tomlinson (1991), Ryan Seacrest (1974), Stephenie Meyer (1973), Ricky Martin (1971), Ed Miliband (1969), Kate Spade (1962), Carol Vorderman (1960), Lemmy Kilmister (1945), Ava Gardner (1922), Howard Hughes (1905), Empress Elisabeth of Austria (1837)

25th December

Hailie Jade (1995), Armin van Buuren (1976), Dido (1971),
Justin Trudeau, Canadian Prime Minister (1971),
Annie Lennox (1954), Sissy Spacek (1949), Jimmy Buffett
(1946), Humphrey Bogart (1899), Muhammad Ali Jinnah,
Founder of Pakistan (1876), Clara Barton (1821)

26th December

Eden Sher (1991), Andy Biersack (1990), Aaron Ramsey (1990),
Kit Harington (1986), Hugo Lloris (1986), Beth Behrs (1985),
Alexander Wang (1983), Jared Leto (1971), Lars Ulrich (1963),
David Sedaris (1956)

27th December

Olivia Cooke (1993), Hayley Williams (1988), Lily Cole (1987),
Emilie de Ravin (1981), Salman Khan (1965), Gérard Depardieu
(1948), John Amos (1939), Marlene Dietrich (1901)

28th December

Sienna Miller (1981), Noomi Rapace (1979), John Legend
(1978), Joe Manganiello (1976), Seth Meyers (1973), Denzel
Washington (1954), Maggie Smith (1934), Stan Lee (1922),
Woodrow Wilson, U.S. President (1856)

29th December

Dylan Minnette (1996), Ross Lynch (1995), Kei Nishikori
(1989), Alison Brie (1982), Charlotte Riley (1981), Diego Luna
(1979), Jude Law (1972), Patricia Clarkson (1959), Ted Danson
(1947), Jon Voight (1938)

PEOPLE WHO SHARE YOUR SIGN
. . . .

30th December

Ellie Goulding (1986), LeBron James (1984), Kristin Kreuk (1982), Eliza Dushku (1980), Tyrese Gibson (1978), Tiger Woods (1975), Patti Smith (1946), Rudyard Kipling (1865)

31st December

Sam Faiers (1990), PSY (1977), Donald Trump Jr. (1977), Nicholas Sparks (1965), Val Kilmer (1959), Donna Summer (1948), Diane von Fürstenberg (1946), John Denver (1943), Ben Kingsley (1943), Alex Ferguson (1941), Anthony Hopkins (1937), King Salman of Saudi Arabia (1935), Henri Matisse (1869)

1st January

Jack Wilshere (1992), Colin Morgan (1986), Paolo Guerrero (1984), Elin Nordegren (1980), Sonali Bendre (1975), Morris Chestnut (1969), Verne Troyer (1969), J.D. Salinger (1919), J. Edgar Hoover (1895)

2nd January

Bryson Tiller (1993), Shelley Hennig (1987), Kate Bosworth (1983), Dax Shepard (1975), Taye Diggs (1971), Christy Turlington (1969), Cuba Gooding Jr. (1968), Tia Carrere (1967)

3rd January

Danica McKellar (1975), Michael Schumacher (1969), Mel Gibson (1956), Victoria Principal (1950), Robert Loggia (1930), Sergio Leone (1929), J. R. R. Tolkien (1892), Savitribai Phule (1831)

4th January

Liza Soberano (1998), Toni Kroos (1990), James Milner
(1986), Jeannie Mai (1979), Julia Ormond (1965), Craig Revel
Horwood (1965), Dave Foley (1963), Harlan Coben (1962),
Michael Stipe (1960), Tina Knowles (1954), Rick Stein (1947)

5th January

Suki Waterhouse (1992), Kristin Cavallari (1987), Deepika
Padukone (1986), Deadmau5 (1981), January Jones (1978),
Bradley Cooper (1975), Marilyn Manson (1969), Vinnie Jones
(1965), Diane Keaton (1946), Hayao Miyazaki (1941)

6th January

MattyBRaps (2003), Irina Shayk (1986), Alex Turner (1986),
Kate McKinnon (1984), Eddie Redmayne (1982), Norman
Reedus (1969), Nigella Lawson (1960), Kahlil Gibran (1883)

7th January

Eden Hazard (1991), Hardwell (1988), Lewis Hamilton (1985),
Lauren Cohan (1982), Vybz Kartel (1976), Jeremy Renner
(1971), Irrfan Khan (1967), Nicolas Cage (1964), Christian
Louboutin (1963)

8th January

Noah Cyrus (2000), David Bowie (1947), Stephen Hawking
(1942), Carolina Herrera (1939), Shirley Bassey (1937),
Elvis Presley (1935)

9th January

Nicola Peltz (1995), Nina Dobrev (1989), Kate Middleton, Duchess of Cambridge (1982), Omari Hardwick (1974), Sean Paul (1973), Joely Richardson (1965), J. K. Simmons (1955), Jimmy Page (1944), Richard Nixon, U.S. President (1913), Simone de Beauvoir (1908)

10th January

Abbey Clancy (1986), Jared Kushner (1981), Cash Warren (1979), Jemaine Clement (1974), Maurizio Sarri (1959), Pat Benatar (1953), George Foreman (1949), Rod Stewart (1945)

11th January

Cody Simpson (1997), Leroy Sané (1996), Jamie Vardy (1987), Rachel Riley (1986), Amanda Peet (1972), Mary J. Blige (1971), Kyle Richards (1969), Yolanda Hadid (1964), Alice Paul (1885)

12th January

Zayn Malik (1993), Naya Rivera (1987), Raf Simons (1968), Rob Zombie (1965), Jeff Bezos (1964), Howard Stern (1954), Kirstie Alley (1951), Haruki Murakami (1949), Swami Vivekananda (1863)

13th January

Liam Hemsworth (1990), Julian Morris (1983), Ruth Wilson (1982), Orlando Bloom (1977), Michael Peña (1976), Nicole Eggert (1972), Patrick Dempsey (1966), Julia Louis-Dreyfus (1961), Janet Hubert (1956)

14th January

Grant Gustin (1990), Yandel (1977), Jason Bateman (1969),
Dave Grohl (1969), LL Cool J (1968), Zakk Wylde (1967),
Carl Weathers (1948), Holland Taylor (1943)

15th January

Dove Cameron (1996), Skrillex (1988), Kelly Kelly (1987),
Pitbull (1981), Regina King (1971), Shane McMahon (1970),
Martin Luther King Jr. (1929)

16th January

FKA twigs (1988), Nick Valensi (1981), Lin-Manuel Miranda
(1980), Aaliyah (1979), Kate Moss (1974), Roy Jones Jr. (1969),
John Carpenter (1948), René Angélil (1942)

17th January

Calvin Harris (1984), Ray J (1981), Zooey Deschanel (1980),
Tiësto (1969), Michelle Obama (1964), Jim Carrey (1962),
Muhammad Ali (1942), James Earl Jones (1931), Betty White
(1922), Al Capone (1899)

18th January

Karan Brar (1999), Angelique Kerber (1988), Jason Segel
(1980), Pep Guardiola (1971), Dave Bautista (1969), Mark
Rylance (1960), Kevin Costner (1955), Cary Grant (1904)

19th January

Logan Lerman (1992), Mac Miller (1992), Claudio Marchisio (1986), Utada Hikaru (1983), Jenson Button (1980), Ricardo Arjona (1964), Dolly Parton (1946), Janis Joplin (1943), Edgar Allan Poe (1809)

20th January

Evan Peters (1987), Joe Swash (1982), Mark Wright (1981), Gary Barlow (1971), Stacey Dash (1967), Rainn Wilson (1966), Bill Maher (1956), Paul Stanley (1952), David Lynch (1946), Dorothy Provine (1935), Tom Baker (1934), Buzz Aldrin (1930), Federico Fellini (1920)